SPAIN
The MONOCLE Handbook

MONOCLE

First published in the United Kingdom in 2023
by MONOCLE and Thames & Hudson Ltd,
181a High Holborn, London, WC1V 7QX
thamesandhudson.com

First published in the United States of America in 2023
by MONOCLE and Thames & Hudson Inc,
500 Fifth Avenue, New York, New York, 10110
thamesandhudsonusa.com

MONOCLE is a trading name of Winkontent Limited

© 2023 Winkontent Limited of Midori House,
1 Dorset Street, London, W1U 4EG

All Rights Reserved. No part of this publication may be reproduced or transmitted in any form or by any means, electronic or mechanical, including photocopy, recording or any other information storage and retrieval system, without prior permission in writing from the publishers. This book is sold subject to the condition that it shall not, by way of trade or otherwise, be lent, re-sold, hired out or otherwise without the publishers' prior consent, in any form of binding or cover other than that in which it is published, and without a similar condition including this condition being imposed on the subsequent purchaser.

British Library Cataloguing-in-Publication Data
A catalogue record for this book is available from
The British Library

Library of Congress Control Number: 2022951163

For more information, please visit *monocle.com*

This book was printed on paper certified
according to the standards of the FSC®

Designed by MONOCLE
Proofreading by MONOCLE
Typeset in Plantin

Printed in Italy by Graphicom
ISBN 978-0-500-97867-2

Cover images
Front cover (from left)
Gambas a la plancha by Ben Roberts;
Espai Xavier Corberó by Anna Huix

Back cover (clockwise from top left)
Beach dining by Salva Lopez; Casa Gonzalez & Gonzalez by Víctor Garrido; Torres Blancas entrance hall by Salva Lopez; Hotel Alfonso XIII by Ben Roberts

Spain

DISCOVER SPAIN
PART 01

We've traversed the country from Bilbao to Barcelona (and dropped anchor in the Canary and Balearic Islands) to find the people and places worth writing home about. Discover the family-run restaurants turning out the tastiest paella and meet the creatives making everything from espadrilles to blankets. We'll take you on a tour of the nation's most striking architecture, visit boundary-pushing museums and maybe even plant our parasol at some of our favourite beaches. *Vamos!*

006—007
Introduction

008—009
Map

010—011
Need to know

WHERE TO STAY

015—021
Coastal hotels

022—027
Rural hotels

028—037
Urban hotels

038—039
The experts

DRINKING & DINING

041—061
Restaurants

062—063
Bakeries

064—065
Sweet treats

066—069
Cafés & speciality coffee

070—071
Wineries

072—079
Bars & drink producers

080—083
Markets

084—085
The experts

DESIGN & RETAIL

087—093
Textiles, lighting & ceramics

094—099
Specialist shops

100—101
Concept stores

102—111
Fashion & shoes

112—113
The experts

114—121
The shopping list

CULTURE

123—133
Museums

134—135
Cultural centres

136—137
Art galleries

138—139
Live music

140—141
Bookshops

142—143
The experts

ARCHITECTURE

145—155
Buildings

THE GREAT OUTDOORS

157—161
Natural parks

162—167
Beaches

CONTENTS

PUT DOWN ROOTS
PART 02

So you've fallen in love with Spain? Perhaps it's time to extend your stay – maybe even permanently. In this chapter we will show you the best spots to set up shop, introduce you to the architects and designers that can help turn your dream into a reality and peek inside a couple of Spanish homes along the way. We also hear from the plucky entrepreneurs who have already made the move.

---

170 — 177
Where to live

178 — 183
Residences

184 — 187
Architecture & design

188 — 189
Furniture

190 — 191
Build a network

192 — 193
Success stories

THE ADDRESS BOOK
PART 03

Use this handy guide to help plan your next trip. Here we present all of our favourite places to stay, eat, shop and visit organised by region. Whether you're heading to Madrid or Mallorca, we've got you covered.

---

196 — 198
Madrid

199
Central

200 — 202
Barcelona

203
Cataluña

204 — 205
Valencia

206
The East

207 — 208
Andalucía

209 — 212
The North

213 — 214
Balearic Islands

215
Canary Islands

218 — 221
Index

222
Acknowledgements

223
About Monocle

Whether you're visiting for a sunny weekend or planning to stay a little longer, *Spain: The Monocle Handbook* makes the perfect travel companion. What are you waiting for?

INTRODUCTION

ANDREW TUCK
Editor in Chief

Thanks to the incredible success of its package holiday industry, Spain became known to many outsiders just as a place of sun, sea and sangria (with flamenco for entertainment). While all the above are things that we love, this version of the nation became so dominant that it often deterred people from experiencing the cooler, wilder shores of say Galicia or heading into the country's interior to discover regions such as Extremadura. But in recent years, Spain has done a fine job of telling more varied stories, enticing people to explore – whether for a few days on a sunny isle, a cross-country road trip or to put down roots in a city on the rise (hello Málaga, Vigo and Valencia).

That's why we wanted to create *Spain: The Monocle Handbook*. We thought it was high time to help more people discover the richness of the country, to taste the differences in cuisines across the regions, to experience the shifts in architecture and culture as you journey from mountain to shore. The MONOCLE Handbook series is designed for travellers like you who want to step away from the milling crowds to track down a tapas joint that the locals swear by, a hotel that makes the most of its setting, a beach where the living is easy and a *chiringuito* bar is never far away. But this book is also for those for whom the pull of Spain is even stronger – for those who want to start a business here, find a place to call home, to simply stay put. So, over the coming pages, we will tell you all of our favourite places in the country, spots for fleeting and life-long experiences.

And we call it a Handbook for a good reason – we want you to really use this book. So throw it in your suitcase, turn over the corners on pages that feature places that you must experience. In short, let us help you see this dynamic, creative, exciting, incredibly diverse country afresh.

MAP

Spain as we know it has only really existed since 1492. It was then that the Christian kingdoms of Castile and Aragon conquered Granada, the last Muslim stronghold, and brought 800 years of Islamic rule in the south to an end. This marked the foundation of modern Spain as a united state but regional identities remain remarkably strong to this day. The country is made up of 17 autonomous regions (including the Canary Islands in the Atlantic Ocean and the Balearic Islands in the Mediterranean), and two autonomous cities in northern Africa: Ceuta and Melilla.

Spain is a mosaic of customs and cuisines shaped by the cultures that have inhabited particular regions over the centuries, including the Celts, Romans and Moors. Even the landscapes shift dramatically as you move from the craggy, verdant coast of the north through the sprawling plains of the centre to the imposing desert scapes and white sandy beaches of the south.

Madrid & central
Spain's capital sits in the centre of a vast plateau known as the Meseta.

The north
The Atlantic coast to the north is wild, craggy and green.

Barcelona & Cataluña
This northeastern region is home to the country's most-visited city.

Valencia & the east
The coastline of Valencia and Murcia is lined with resorts.

Andalucía
Evidence of the region's Moorish past can be found everywhere you look.

Balearic Islands
These Mediterranean islands have long drawn sun worshippers.

Canary Islands
This sub-tropical archipelago of eight islands sits just off the coast of Africa.

THE BALEARIC ISLANDS

MAP

THE MAINLAND

THE CANARY ISLANDS

NEED TO KNOW

We turn a spotlight on the nation's traditions and quirks, from the way its people enjoy their food (locally sourced and shared with friends) to lessons in community and pace of life.

THE DAY'S SCHEDULE
Life of leisure

Days unfold slowly in Spain, with the clock adhering to human rhythms rather than the other way around. Relaxed starts are the norm as Spaniards stay up well past dinnertime, making it a challenge to rise early for breakfast. Those with jobs that require a prompt start can most often be found at the nearest cafeteria around 10:30 enjoying *un café de media mañana*, a snack and catch-up with colleagues designed to see them through to lunch. The slower Spanish pace allows time for recharging and enjoying life's simple pleasures: independent businesses close in the middle of the day, while restaurants shutter between lunch and dinner services, for siesta. The length of time this midday break lasts is something many disagree on. The rule seems to depend on how much wine you've had with lunch, what day of the week it is, what plans you have for the evening ahead and whether it's summer – siesta times increase exponentially with hot weather. Once you've walked a deserted street in the unbearable heat, you'll soon realise the practicality behind this afternoon pause.

FIESTAS
Party people

Spaniards never miss a chance to celebrate, with individual holidays as well as days-long fiestas held throughout the year in honour of everything from saints to livestock. In fact, there isn't a week that goes by in the summer without a party going on in some corner of the country. Many stem from the Catholic Church, however non-religious festivals – such as Valencia's La Tomatina, a massive tomato-based food fight – capture the joyful irreverence central to most events. Regional foods share the limelight in these revelries. During summer fiestas (which have pre-Christian roots), the rich excesses of *chocolate con churros* (fried dough with chocolate) make an appearance in temporary stalls. On many occasions the cultural focus shifts entirely to a particular dish. For example, Cataluña's Gran Festa de la Calçotada celebrates spring onions roasted over open flames, while in the Basque village of Getaria an open-air competition is held to find the town's best *marmitako*, longfin-tuna stew.

NIGHTLIFE
The late show

Perfect for night owls, the country's nightlife typically extends into the early morning. After dinner (which generally doesn't get going until 22:00), the focus shifts to chatting over drinks. Spaniards are excellent at pacing themselves, as *la noche* is treated as a marathon where alcoholic drinks are imbibed moderately – parties don't tend to reach their peak until the sun rises. In the south, don't be surprised to hear the strains of flamenco (and couples jumping into spontaneous dance) at any time of the day or night. Ibiza may be world-renowned for its DJ-led nights but all of Spain's larger cities offer a wide range of clubs and after-hours bars. And as party-goers are turfed-out, they often grab a bite to eat: Madrileños' breakfast of champions is a calamari sandwich consumed as the day dawns.

GETTING AROUND
All aboard

The Alta Velocidad Española (Spanish High Speed Rail) is known colloquially by its acronym – AVE (ah-veh) – a play on *ave*, the Spanish word for bird. In fact, passengers might actually feel as though they've taken flight when trains reach their top speed of 310km/h. Locals make frequent use of the railway as the network links many cities that may not be connected by air. And taking in the dramatic landscapes that zip past the panoramic windows is a far superior experience to driving. *Preferente*, Ave's first-class service, comes complete with a complimentary newspaper and glass of cava – offering an experience akin to the golden age of flying.

REGIONS
Time to explore

Spain's 17 regions each reflect strong cultural and historical identities and a number of them have their own additional languages. From the verdant mountains of Asturias to the subtropical shores of the Canary Islands, Spain's varied geography is an incomparable patchwork made all the richer by its history. Modern-day Navarre, for example, corresponds almost completely with its medieval territory when it was known as the Kingdom of Navarre. And while Spain's State of Autonomies recognises its regions' cultural individuality, the act of coming together as a nation has not always been easy. Separatist movements in the Basque Country and Cataluña have challenged the central government in the past, though all sides are keen to avoid a repeat of the historical violence.

HISTORY
Storied past

The Iberian peninsula's strategic position at the intersection of Europe, Africa, the Mediterranean and the Atlantic has attracted settlers as varied as the Phoenicians, Romans, Visigoths and Celts. And so this land became multicultural before the term even existed. Muslim dynasties ruled much of the peninsula for almost eight centuries, with the major cities of Al-Ándalus (the Arabic term for Iberia), such as Córdoba, rising to become Europe's most populous and most learned. In the 16th century, the kingdoms that would become modern-day Spain ushered in an era of European colonisation of the Americas. Since then, the shifting tides of fortune have seen Spaniards and Latin Americans migrate back and forth across the ocean, with cultural and linguistic links facilitating their journeys. In recent years, Latin Americans have contributed to a rich local fabric as the country's largest immigrant group. The scars of the civil war (1936–1939) and the following dictatorship that marked much of the 20th century in Spain, make this period a sensitive subject. Spaniards will rarely bring up the war, or Franco, themselves, so it should be a fairly easy task to avoid inadvertently injuring sensibilities.

EATING
Table talk

A common expression in Spain is *"donde comen dos, comen tres"*, which roughly translates to "if there's enough food for two, there's enough for three". This phrase reveals a hospitality founded in the belief that meals should be savoured in company – that there is always room to welcome one more to the table. The traditional family Sunday lunch continues to be the foundation of Spain's celebratory dining spirit. When eating out informally Spaniards order large portions such as patatas bravas or *pulpo a la gallega* (Galician-style octopus) that are shared among a group. These plates pass from hand to hand around the table, with people eating a bit here and there between laughs and glasses of wine. The boisterous socialising that takes place is almost as important as the bountiful servings themselves. Take *sobremesa* (which means "over the table"), which describes the Spanish marathon of chit-chat interspersed with sweets and stiff drinks that can stretch on for hours after a meal. Restaurants make room for this custom, with staff often letting diners linger over *chupitos* (shots) of homemade digestifs.

COMMUNITY
It's personal

With family sitting firmly at the centre of community in Spain, it's no surprise that touch is fundamental. Expect to be hugged as part of a regular greeting (with a kiss placed on each cheek), or heartily patted on the back for a job well done. Across Spain, all generations can be seen enjoying each other's company, whether during a Sunday stroll or a meal out. Most Spaniards also have a tight-knit crew of *amigos de toda la vida* (lifelong friends) that acts as an extended family. Every outing becomes a fun-filled opportunity to assemble one's large group, whether going out for a hike or celebrating a football victory. With community and human connection as priorities, no one is ever in too much of a rush to stop and chat when someone they know crosses their path – be they friend, neighbour or the local fishmonger.

PART 01

DISCOVER SPAIN

Take a tour of the country's best hospitality, design, culture and architecture – plus the beaches and outdoor spaces not to be missed.

Beautifully restored historic buildings, beachside boltholes and sleek inner-city spots – whether you're travelling for business or pleasure, here's our guide to Spain's best hotels.

WHERE TO STAY

As the world's second most-visited country (France just nabs the top spot), Spain offers visitors a wealth of accommodation options. But it's not a case of quantity over quality – the Spanish are famed for their warmth and hospitality and this is reflected in their hotels. Strong regional identities mean your stay will often come with a generous serving of local flavour – from Catalan fare in Barcelona to Moorish influences in the south. You'll also be rewarded for going off the beaten track, where many of the country's most scenic spots still feel refreshingly undiscovered. And while traditional charm is rarely in short supply, a number of young hot-shot hoteliers have injected new life into some of the country's most storied institutions as well as opening up their own design-conscious ventures. To help you make an informed choice, we've collated our favourite options, covering everything from idyllic farm-stays to Mediterranean mansions and stylish urban guesthouses.

THE EDIT

1 Coastal hotels
Parts of Spain's coastline may have been blighted by overdevelopment, but know where to look and you'll find tranquil spots with bucket-loads of charm.

2 Rural hotels
A collection of properties that showcase the best of the Spanish countryside.

3 Urban hotels
From San Sebastián to Seville, discover our pick of the inner-city accommodation options with prime locations.

4 The experts
Meet three hospitality experts who lift the lid on Spain's burgeoning hotel industry.

WHERE TO STAY

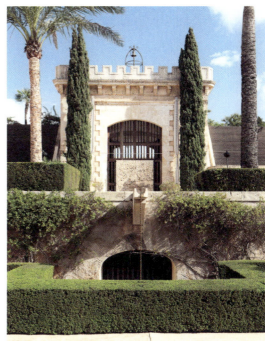

COASTAL HOTEL
CAP ROCAT
Mallorca

Though it's just a 20-minute drive from Palma, Cap Rocat feels a world away from the island's urban centre. Located within a nature reserve, the hotel is set in a converted 19th-century fortress (complete with drawbridge and trenches) that overlooks the protected coastline. Architect Antonio Obrados seamlessly integrated the building's history by converting former artillery positions, where cannons once stood, into the hotel's exclusive Sentinel suites. Carved out of the rock face, each room includes a private pool and terrace, where guests can enjoy breakfast with dramatic sea views.
caprocat.com

Healing powers
At the centre of the fortress is Cap Rocat's hidden jewel: a spa with an indoor salt-water pool chiselled into the fortress's stone walls.

SPAIN

COASTAL HOTEL
SIX SENSES IBIZA
Ibiza

Six Senses Ibiza was designed by architect and owner Jonathan Leitersdorf. As well as 118 rooms, the resort offers 19 luxury residences and two private mansions where guests can enjoy a heightened sense of privacy while taking advantage of the resort's facilities – of which there are many. As well as an impressive spa (with an equally impressive list of treatments), the hotel hosts cooking lessons, yoga, guided tours of the island and more. And those looking for a slice of Ibiza's nightlife won't be disappointed: Six Senses' Beach Caves bar is known for its sundowners and live music.
sixsenses.com

WHERE TO STAY

COASTAL HOTEL
CASA NERETA
Cadaqués, Cataluña

The picturesque Costa Brava town of Cadaqués has long been a favourite retreat for artists – both Picasso and Dalí spent time living here. The latter was a friend of painter Joan Ponç, whose 1950s home in the town is now a 12-room guesthouse run by Ponç's grandson James Pons. The sun-splashed interiors feature white walls and lamps from Santa & Cole. "We also aim to offer a memorable experience when it comes to food," says Pons, who opened the adjoining Bistro Nereta in 2022. Here guests can wash down locally-caught seafood with a glass of Catalan wine.
casanereta.com

Creative community
Known for the quality of its light, Cadaqués attracted some of the biggest names in the 20th-century art world. Aside from Picasso and Dalí, the sleepy fishing town lured the likes of Miró, Matisse, Duchamp and Man Ray.

COASTAL HOTEL
LA BIONDA
Begur, Cataluña

Carla Lloveras opened La Bionda in 2020 in Begur, a small hillside town on the Costa Brava. "When I first saw the property I immediately fell in love with it," she says of the 17th-century building that now houses her eight-room hotel. Lloveras enlisted the help of Barcelona design studio Quintana Partners, which filled the interiors with a playful mix of vintage finds and bespoke furnishings, including cane chairs, fringed lampshades and free-standing bathtubs. Don't miss the breakfast: Lloveras, who comes from a family of butchers, serves charcuterie from her parents' shop alongside fresh bread that she picks up every morning. *labiondabegur.com*

WHERE TO STAY

COASTAL HOTEL
MARBELLA CLUB
Marbella, Andalucía

In 1954, Prince Alfonso of Hohenlohe-Langenburg turned his family holiday home into a hub for the jet set, including golden-age Hollywood stars such as Audrey Hepburn and Grace Kelly. The prince's vision would transform Marbella from a humble fishing village into a lavish retreat on par with Biarritz and Monaco. Though today the Costa del Sol is anything but undiscovered, the Marbella Club retains an air of discreet glamour thanks to its attentive service and sprawling botanical gardens. The property has 115 rooms and suites plus 17 villas scattered across the grounds.
marbellaclub.com

Spoilt for choice
The hotel offers guests nine drinking and dining options, from pool-side to beach-side, breakfast spots to fine dining. Most famous is El Grill, which specialises in grilled meat and fish.

COASTAL HOTEL
AKELARRE
San Sebastián

Akelarre hotel opened in 2017 but its story starts nearly five decades (and three Michelin stars) earlier with Akelarre restaurant, launched by chef Pedro Subijana in the 1970s. The establishment's rural location on the slopes of Mount Igeldo inspired Subijana to open a hotel where his diners could stay the night following a meal in the restaurant. Oihana, Subijana's daughter, now heads up the hotel which boasts slick interiors courtesy of Madrid-based studio Mecanismo. Each of the 22 rooms command impressive views over the Bay of Biscay.
akelarre.net

The tastemakers
Pedro Subijana was a founding member of the Gang of Twelve: a group of chefs who took cues from nouvelle cuisine in France and redefined Basque cooking in the 1970s, today known as *nueva cocina vasca*.

COASTAL HOTEL
GRAN HOTEL LA TOJA
La Toja, Galicia

COASTAL HOTEL
HACIENDA CUATRO VENTANAS
Tenerife

Hidden among banana plantations on the northwest coast of Tenerife is this restored 17th-century property. With six sleek villas, sprawling gardens and infinity pool, Hacienda Cuatro Ventanas proves that there is more to the island's hospitality offering than the concrete developments and package holidays that made it famous in the 1970s. Owner Alberto del Hoyo, who was born on Tenerife, returned after 20 years in Madrid to open the hotel on his family's estate. "The house was falling into disrepair," he says. "I wanted to give it a new life while showing the community that it was possible to shift away from existing hotel models."
haciendacuatroventanas.com

When it first opened its doors in 1907, Gran Hotel La Toja became the world's first resort to offer guests a golf course and spa. It wasn't long until it caught the attention of the rich and famous: Infanta Isabel of Spain, Queen Isabella II's daughter, famously graced its halls. The resort, which can be found on its own island (connected to the mainland by a bridge), has continued to welcome the well-heeled, hosting figures such as David Rockefeller and Gabriel García Márquez. Many guests still come for the spa, which offers thermal waters, a sauna and massage treatments. Don't miss the hotel's three restaurants which serve classic Galician dishes.
eurostarshotels.co.uk

SPAIN

RURAL HOTEL
MENORCA EXPERIMENTAL
Menorca

This playfully renovated hotel by Experimental can be found in a *finca* deep in the Menorca countryside. The hospitality group (which came to the fore with a glitzy cocktail club and has hotels in Ibiza, New York and Verbier) is known for its impeccable taste in design and gastronomy – and this island bolthole is no different. The interior is dotted with native touches, bright colours and furniture made by local artisans. As well as a private pool, the hotel offers access to a quiet cove. "It's a place to slow down and disconnect," says co-owner Pierre-Charles Cros.
menorcaexperimental.com

Mix it up
In true Experimental style, the hotel's culinary offering is one of its main draws – expect a menu of modern Mediterranean fare cooked with produce from the kitchen garden and local suppliers.

WHERE TO STAY

RURAL HOTEL
ES RACÓ D'ARTÀ
Mallorca

Friends Antoni Esteva and Jaume Danús are the duo behind this minimalist retreat. Set on one of Mallorca's largest rural estates, surrounded by vineyards and almond and olive groves, the 13th-century farmhouse was renovated by Esteva, who is also an architect. The main house, with its old stone walls and wooden beams, offers eight rooms, with an additional 21 small houses across the estate. Rooms are furnished with simple wooden furniture, basketry and ceramics by Mallorquín artisans. The restaurant serves dishes made from the organic produce from the working farm.
esracodarta.com

RURAL HOTEL
PARADOR DE SEGOVIA
Segovia, Castilla y León

Storied stays
The Paradores group has 97 unique establishments – in buildings which range from castles to convents – many of which play a key role in revitalising the economic and social activity of Spain's most depopulated regions.

Paradores de Turismo de España is a group of hotels with almost a century's worth of hospitality expertise. Whereas most of its properties are housed in converted historical buildings, the Parador de Segovia was purpose-built as a hotel in 1978. Architect Joaquín Pallás employed a fan-like brutalist design that capitalised on the location's panoramic views of Segovia's old town, now a UNESCO World Heritage Site. During cooler months, visitors can relax by one of the hotel's suspended fireplaces or perhaps take a dip in the circular indoor pool.
parador.es

WHERE TO STAY

RURAL HOTEL
ABADÍA RETUERTA LEDOMAINE
Valladolid, Castilla y León

RURAL HOTEL
VILLA RIU BLANC
Jávea, Valencia

Set among the hills of Benissa on the coast north of Benidorm is Villa Riu Blanc, a vibrant five-suite guesthouse that lawyers-turned-hoteliers Patricia and Dirk Huygens-Rommens opened in 2022. The pair transformed the former farmhouse into a tranquil retreat peppered with pops of Mediterranean colour, handmade ceramics, eclectic artworks and cosy furnishings.
"Villa Riu Blanc is not your typical *finca*," says Patricia. "The design was inspired by Kandinsky's concept that 'Colour is a power which directly influences the soul.'" Alongside its striking interiors, the hotel offers a secluded swimming pool and serves a hearty breakfast.
villariublanc.es

Abadía Retuerta LeDomaine is housed in a monastery once run by wine-making monks in the 12th century – a tradition the hotel has continued with an award-winning winery that offers seven types of red and white. With only 27 rooms and three suites, the abbey is spacious and quiet with wide stone corridors and interior courtyards. It also boasts an impressive art collection, which includes "Rumor de Límites V" by Basque sculptor Eduardo Chillida. Chef Marc Segarra is behind the hotel's Michelin-starred restaurant, set in the refectory where the monks once shared their meals.
abadia-retuerta.com

RURAL HOTEL
PLAZA 18
Vejer de la Frontera, Andalucía

RURAL HOTEL
FINCA LA DONAIRA
Montecorto, Andalucía

This country estate, located among the *pueblos blancos* (white towns) of Andalucía's Grazalema Mountains, covers some 700 hectares. "This place has a very raw energy," explains founder Manfred Bodner, who took over the land in 2005 with plans to reforest the area. The nine-room *finca* comprises an equestrian stable, a spring-fed pool, a spa and an organic farm from which Michelin-star-chef Fredrik Andersson develops daily menus. Bodner (originally from Austria) hopes that La Donaira can be a space for those seeking balance. "We really try to combine the good things of urban culture and relocate them to a rural environment," he says.
ladonaira.com

Off the whitewashed Plaza de España in Vejer de la Frontera, James Stuart and Regli Álvarez have created a series of hotels that function like a village within a village to highlight the town's labyrinthine quality. "Rather than building from scratch, we have been able to reuse housing and support growth in the old town," says Stuart. The project has since incorporated buildings that date back to the 13th century. In 2019 the duo opened the luxurious Plaza 18, a six-bedroom property in a restored 19th-century townhouse. With an honesty bar and oil paintings, Plaza 18 feels less like a hotel and more like a lavish private home.
califavejer.com/plaza-18

WHERE TO STAY

RURAL HOTEL
CASA JOSEPHINE
Sorzano, La Rioja

Iñigo Aragón and Pablo López Navarro founded their studio Casa Josephine (*see page 186*) in 2012 and soon established themselves as one of Madrid's most sought-after design talents. This five-bedroom guesthouse near Logroño in La Rioja's wine region was their first foray into the hospitality sector. The result is a house that exemplifies their rustic but considered aesthetic, which mixes furniture from different periods and styles and ultimately prioritises the comfort of their guests. "We wanted to create a place that echoes the relaxed spirit of family summer houses," says López Navarro.
casajosephine.com

SPAIN

URBAN HOTEL
ROSEWOOD VILLA MAGNA
Madrid

Prime spot
The hotel's location between the elegant Chamberí and Salamanca neighbourhoods makes it an ideal base for exploring the city on foot. The site also backs onto El Corte Inglés department store – perfect for guests who want to hit the shops.

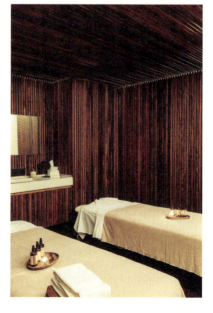

Upon its original inauguration in 1972, the Villa Magna became an iconic standard-bearer of luxury in the capital. With its reopening in 2021, under the stewardship of the Rosewood Hotel Group, this legacy has served as a touchstone in the contemporary redesign. What had been a staid concrete façade (considered avant-garde in its day) has gained light and movement through a black-and-gold modular intervention by architect Ramón de Arana. This continues inside where several restaurants tempt guests including Amós by Jesús Sánchez, one of Spain's top chefs.
rosewoodhotels.com

URBAN HOTEL
THE MADRID EDITION
Madrid

The Edition hotel group opened its new Madrid iteration in April 2022. With views of the Plaza de las Descalzas, the hotel is located close to Puerta del Sol and Plaza Mayor but the rooftop pool and terrace bar could trick you into thinking you were on the Mediterranean. The interior was designed by British architect John Pawson and Paris-based François Champsaur. The result is rather sophisticated: the 200 rooms flaunt an elegant scheme in shades of white, with standout pieces including the bespoke bar furnishings and striking spiral staircase.
editionhotels.com/madrid

URBAN HOTEL
GRAN HOTEL INGLÉS
Madrid

Holding the title of the oldest hotel in Madrid, the 48-room Gran Inglés blends its own (significant) history with art deco design and contemporary comforts. Located in the central Barrio de las Letras neighbourhood, the hotel's legacy stretches back to the mid-19th century when it was a speakeasy. Hotel Inglés enjoyed a few decades as a watering hole for the creative elite (visited by the likes of Virginia Woolf and Ernest Hemingway) but eventually fell into disrepair. It underwent a five-year renovation, re-emerging as a beacon of luxury in 2018. But there's still a hint of the hotel's storied past: on the ground floor, a dimly lit 1920s-era bar serves cocktails and tapas.
granhotelingles.com

URBAN HOTEL
COTTON HOUSE
Barcelona

Cotton House hotel sits within a stately 19th-century mansion that was built as a home for the aristocratic Boada family. It functioned as the headquarters of the Cotton Textile Guild before opening its doors as a hotel in 2015 with interiors courtesy of Catalan designer Lázaro Rosa Violán. "The frescoes on the ceilings and the parquet floors have all been maintained," says general manager Natalia de la Fuente. Newly-added elements include a rooftop pool with views across the Eixample neighbourhood all the way to the Sagrada Familia.
hotelcottonhouse.com

WHERE TO STAY

URBAN HOTEL
CASA BONAY
Barcelona

Barcelona's Casa Bonay occupies a 1869 townhouse overlooking the tree-lined avenue of Gran Via. More than just a place for visitors to rest their head, hotelier Inés Miró-Sans has created something of a community hub for the city's creative crowd. Locals can drop by for negronis and live DJ sets at the Libertine bar, flat whites at Satan's Coffee Corner café and dinner at adjoining restaurant Bodega. "Casa Bonay is a place where people can swing by whenever they want," says Miró Sans. "They feel welcome. It's a home away from home for many people."
casabonay.com

Good neighbours
Local collaborations were at the heart of Miró-Sans' philosophy. Much of the furniture is by Poblenou-based AOO, the playful wallpaper and cushions are by Batabasta and light fixtures come courtesy of Santa & Cole.

URBAN HOTEL
YOURS BOUTIQUE HOTEL
Valencia

Dutch couple Daphne Kniest and Wouter Kock opened 12-key boutique hotel Yours in 2020. "After a thorough search for the perfect building, our eyes fell on an old laundrette," says Kniest. "It was close to the historical centre but in the exciting neighbourhood of Ruzafa." They worked with architecture studio Eseiesa on the renovation before taking the interior design into their own hands. Valencian furniture brand Viccarbe and lighting company Arkoslight helped to create a luminous, pared-back design that matches whitewashed walls with contemporary furnishings. On hot days, guests can cool off in the plunge pool in the tropical courtyard.
thisisyours.es

URBAN HOTEL
PLÁCIDO Y GRATA
Seville

Marta Santana, a trained architect and co-founder of Barcelona-based interior design studio Your Living Space, opened this 15-room hotel in her hometown of Seville in 2021. The 19th-century manor house needed extensive renovations: Santana opted for pared-back Scandinavian-inspired interiors with a neutral colour palette – a far cry from the maximalist aesthetic the city tends to favour. On the ground floor there is a sleek coffee shop which sources beans from Nomad Coffee (*see page 68*) and across the road you'll find La Tienda – a restaurant and retail space from the Plácido y Grata team – both open to non-guests.
placidoygratahotel.com

URBAN HOTEL
HOTEL ALFONSO XIII
Seville

Commissioned by the King of Spain – who felt inclined to lend it his name – to host dignitaries visiting for the Ibero-American Exhibition in 1929, this Seville landmark had one simple ambition: to become the grandest hotel in Europe. Almost a century later (and now part of the Marriott's Luxury Collection) Alfonso XIII is not resting on its laurels. The hotel is still known for its impeccable service and has seamlessly incorporated new technologies and comforts into its traditional architecture, which fuses Andalucian, Moorish and Castilian styles.
theluxurycollection.com/seville

SPAIN

URBAN HOTEL
HOTEL ARBASO
Sän Sebastián

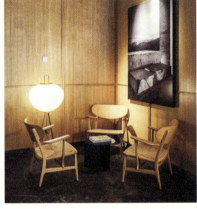

Neighbourhood watch
The Centro area hasn't always been the most desired in San Sebastián – it has had to contend with the *pintxo*-packed Old Town and youthful Gros district. But Arbaso is one of a number of businesses shaking up the area.

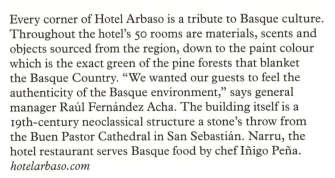

Every corner of Hotel Arbaso is a tribute to Basque culture. Throughout the hotel's 50 rooms are materials, scents and objects sourced from the region, down to the paint colour which is the exact green of the pine forests that blanket the Basque Country. "We wanted our guests to feel the authenticity of the Basque environment," says general manager Raúl Fernández Acha. The building itself is a 19th-century neoclassical structure a stone's throw from the Buen Pastor Cathedral in San Sebastián. Narru, the hotel restaurant serves Basque food by chef Iñigo Peña.
hotelarbaso.com

WHERE TO STAY

URBAN HOTEL
GRAN HOTEL DOMINE BILBAO
Bilbao

Overlooking the Guggenheim Museum Bilbao (*see page 127*), this luxury hotel is itself a work of art. The building's design was originally conceived by Javier Mariscal, a Spanish artist and designer whose colourful pieces can be found throughout the building, including "Fossil Cypress" a towering sculpture displayed in the hotel's atrium. In addition to its prime location in the arts district, Gran Hotel Domine boasts a roof terrace with views of not only the museum but also the Río Nervión. As might be expected in this gastonomic destination, there are a number of dining options, including Beltz restaurant, Le Café and Sixty-One bar.
hoteldominebilbao.com

URBAN HOTEL
HOTEL PALACIO ICO
Lanzarote

Although it lost its status as Lanzarote's capital in the 19th century, Teguise has retained much of its charm and the town is known for its whitewashed colonial architecture. One of the most impressive examples is now home to the Palacio Ico – a nine-room hotel in a building that dates back to the 1690s. As with many stuctures on the island, the property wraps around a courtyard and boasts original features such as coffered ceilings, teak flooring and stone walls more than half a metre thick. Recent additions such as sinks carved from the island's volcanic stone and furniture by local artisans lend the hotel a more contemporary touch.
hotelpalacioico.com

URBAN HOTEL
CAN BORDOY
Mallorca

Mallorca has a plethora of polished architecture (and some overdone monstrosities too) but Can Bordoy stands out. This Mallorquín palace has been turned into Palma's most talked-about hotel by local architects Jaime Oliver and Paloma Hernaiz of Ohlab (*see page 184*) with the wise guidance of Swedish owner Mikael Hall. There are 24 guest rooms filled with a mix of modern furniture and antiques, rich velvet curtains that hide and encase, and cocktail cabinets designed for the project. There's a lush garden with a small pool, a spa and a sharp bar and restaurant. *canbordoy.com*

WHERE TO STAY

URBAN HOTEL
ATRIO
Cáceres, Extremadura

Top table
Guests are given preference when reserving a table at the hotel's Michelin-star restaurant, which boasts what is arguably the best wine cellar in the country.

Cáceres natives Juan Antonio Pérez and José Polo have spent decades putting their beloved city on the map. They first launched Atrio in 1986 as a stand-alone restaurant. In 2010, with the help of architects Mansilla & Tuñón, the pair relaunched Atrio as a restaurant-hotel bringing modern flair to the medieval walled city. In the 14-room property (part of the luxury group Relais & Châteaux), Pérez and Polo have added personal touches, such as decorating the space with art from their own collection – including a Warhol – making the hotel feel particularly welcoming.
restauranteatrio.com

Tourism has long played an important role in Spain's economy (Benidorm, we're looking at you) but the scene has evolved to include a wealth of first-class hotels. We speak to three people in the industry.

MEET THE EXPERTS

HOTELIER
PABLO CARRINGTON
Marugal

Pablo Carrington is the founder of hotel management group Marugal, which runs Cap Rocat (*see page 15*).

How do you view the hospitality industry in Spain?
There are lots of opportunities here – in fact, few countries in Europe can rival the Spanish climate, our natural landscapes, and the cultural and gastronomic offerings. Often it's about building new hotels, but we should be converting existing ones. There are many outdated mid-range hotels from the 1960s and 1970s that need new concepts and renovations. As an industry, we need to move away from mass tourism and towards a more sustainable approach.

What are the challenges of running a hotel in Spain?
Seasonality remains an issue in certain regions, which means that you have to be able to operate a profitable hotel that closes for four or five months of the year.

What advice would you give to a new hotelier?
Regardless of the price or positioning, make sure that you have a distinct concept that offers a differentiated stay for your guests – so many hotels offer a standardised, mass-produced experience these days. I would also advise you to look beyond obvious destinations – Spain has many untapped spots, such as La Rioja, Huelva and Castilla y León.

HOTEL MANAGER
ÉLIDA SUÁREZ MUIÑOS
El Môderne Hotel

HOTELIER
JAVIER CORTINA
Serawa Hotels

Élida Suárez Muiños has been at the helm of El Môderne in Gijón since it opened in 2018.

Architect and hotelier, Javier Cortina is the founder of Serawa Alicante and Hotel Serawa Moraira.

What is your role at El Môderne?
I take care of the numbers, manage the team and work with clients, making sure they feel comfortable and that I'm listening to them because there are always things to improve. I'm also in constant contact with the owners.

Tell us about how you started in hospitality…
I studied tourism and became a hotel manager of BAL Hotel, which is in Asturias, at 28 years old. I was the manager of a four-star hotel in Ribadesella for four years and then started working with El Môderne in August 2018, four months before the hotel opened.

What were some of the challenges?
The building was built in 1931 (in beautiful art deco style) and was abandoned for 10 years before the hotel reopened, so there was a lot of work to do. It was also difficult to weather the pandemic, since the business was still young when that happened. But probably my most challenging task has been making a team that works well together. There are only 18 employees, so this is very important.

What was the inspiration behind Serawa Hotels?
The idea arose from a project I was working on with my architecture firm Ggarchitects, which specialises in sustainable and contemporary designs. We were developing three hotels in Ibiza when we discovered an interesting opportunity to create a hospitality business with sustainability at its core. My firm collaborated with Antonio Pérez Navarro, a hospitality consultant, to make Serawa Hotels a reality.

How does the hospitality industry in Spain compare to other countries around the world?
We have always been innovative when it comes to tourism. In fact, aside from the US, we have one of the biggest tourism incomes in the world. We are good hosts given our friendly, warm and welcoming character, and we also offer a great climate and gastronomy, which is recognised internationally. But Spain also has good infrastructure and excellent travel connections. We have become the preferred destination for many Europeans.

What sets the Serawa hotels apart?
We want to make a positive impact on our guests, through a unique, environmentally-friendly stay. We have a key sustainability plan – for instance the products in our shop are all sourced from regional makers. We also really focus on the customer experience and pay a lot of attention to the small details.

Tapas, paella, *pintxos* – Spanish cuisine is world renowned. We've totted up our favourite restaurants, cafés, food retailers and bars from Vigo to Valencia so you can see, and taste, for yourself.

DRINKING & DINING

The warmth of a Spanish welcome has much to do with the simple act of breaking bread together. Whether socialising with an aperitivo or ironing out a business deal over a three-course lunch, Spaniards prioritise meeting face-to-face while sharing the pleasures of quality food and drink. Spain also boasts incredible natural resources that produce top-rated raw ingredients: the fish and seafood brought in from its expansive shores has made the capital's Mercamadrid the second-largest fish market in the world. In recent decades, chefs have capitalised on this bounty to rank among the globe's top restaurants. Whether at a seaside shack or a Michelin-starred restaurant, prepare to be embraced by the hospitality and history behind every dish. But enough of dining, what about drinking? As well as a fêted wine industry, Spain also has a history of producing everything from cider and beer to sherry – which might help explain the number of top bars across the country.

THE EDIT

1 Restaurants
A tasty round up of the best Spanish fare, from fine-dining to family-run.

2 Bakeries
Where to source your morning loaf.

3 Sweet treats
Get your sugar fix – from ice-cream in Palma to Valencian delicacy *horchata*.

4 Cafés & speciality coffee
Whether you're after a flat white or *café con leche*, we've got you covered.

5 Wineries
Hit the bottle at three fine vineyards.

6 Bars
From a glitzy roof terrace to an old-school drinking hole, here's our pick of Spain's best bars.

7 Drink producers
A traditional Basque cidery and Galicia's favourite beer label.

7 Markets
Four community hubs that offer fresh, high-quality produce.

8 The experts
The industry insiders on how to succeed in Spanish hospitality.

DRINKING & DINING

RESTAURANT
GRESCA
Barcelona

Chef Rafael Peña cut his teeth at famed restaurant El Bulli as well as some of Spain's other highly regarded institutions before launching his own venture in 2017. With Gresca, his mission is to elevate Catalan cuisine to new heights while keeping it unpretentious. The menu features refined versions of Spanish classics such as confit pork infused with orange and ginger and squid stuffed with black chanterelle mushrooms. Gresca is a restaurant of two parts: one side is reserved for a fine-dining experience while the adjoining wine and tapas bar is a more casual affair.
gresca.rest

RESTAURANT
BALDOMERO
Barcelona

Barcelona's Baldomero may be housed in a former garage but you'd be hard pressed to tell. "I decorated the restaurant as if it were a country house," says Antonella Tignanelli, who was involved in the early phases of the project. Since opening in 2019 the restaurant has become known for its weekend brunches which are served buffet-style at a long wooden table, platters piled high with feta-topped roasted carrots and wild rice infused with lemon, among others. "The menu is a compilation of home-cooked recipes from around the world," says Tignanelli. "It's the kind of comfort food your grandmother might make."
casabaldomero.com

DRINKING & DINING

RESTAURANT
FONDA PEPA
Barcelona

Fonda Pepa has the old-school charm of a restaurant well beyond its years. Opened in 2021 by chefs Pedro Baño and Paco Benítez (*pictured*), it has a traditional brasserie feel with gleaming marble tables and black-and-white tiled floors. There's also an open kitchen where diners can look on as chefs artfully prepare refined-but-hearty Catalan dishes. "Our menu is traditional with a twist," says Benítez. "The idea was to create a neighbourhood restaurant where locals can enjoy fine dining with a casual atmosphere."
fondapepa.com

RESTAURANT
GRANJA VENDRELL
Barcelona

When restaurateur Arianna Grau heard that iconic Barcelona bistro Granja Vendrell was closing after nearly a century, she decided to step in. "It had been run by the Vendrell family for three generations," she explains. "I loved the place and all its history. I wanted to revive the business and its traditions." Grau restored the original art deco signage and interiors, complete with marble panelling, pendant lamps and large mirrors. The menu is updated seasonally and is an unfussy mix of Catalan dishes such as roast duck with braised red cabbage and tomato salad with smoked sardines.
+34 930 112 150

RESTAURANT
NORMAL
Girona, Cataluña

From the owners of award-winning restaurant El Celler de Can Roca comes a second endeavour by brothers Joan, Josep and Jordi Roca – and it is a statement in simplicity. Normal's bare stone walls and minimalist dining room create an atmosphere of calm. Despite the sophisticated interior, the menu itself is rather playful with dishes including pickled mussels with apple and fennel and pumpkin ravioli with truffle. "We wanted to reiterate the essence of eating out, which should be all about proximity, farm-grown, market-sourced produce and the intuition that harks back to our grandparents' way of doing things," says Josep.
restaurantnormal.com

DRINKING & DINING

RESTAURANT
LA PEPICA
Valencia

Just steps from the sand you'll find La Pepica, a centuries-old institution known for turning out one of Valencia's best paellas. The family-run restaurant, which is now in its third generation, started as a makeshift sandwich supplier in 1898. Today the establishment is run by Pepe Balaguer (*pictured, on right*) and his 50-strong team, who regularly attend to some 400 customers each sitting. The storied spot counts popes, royalty and Ernest Hemingway among past punters. "We've survived simply by respecting our grandparents and not changing their time-honoured recipe," says Balaguer.
lapepica.com

Pan out
The word "paella" doesn't refer to the rice dish but rather the pan that it's cooked in, which means you will have to be more specific when ordering. Some establishments serve a dozen or more varieties.

RESTAURANT
OSTRAS PEDRÍN
Valencia

RESTAURANT
LA PLAYA DE MODA
Valencia

The beach bars (or *chiringuitos*) that line Valencia's shores are rarely recognised for their culinary credentials but La Playa de Moda has established itself as a superior place to sample Valencian cuisine. The duo behind the enterprise are restaurateur José Miralles and Hugo Cerverón, who first teamed up to launch Mercabañal, a contemporary food court and cultural space in El Cabanyal. La Playa de Moda diners can sample modern dishes, including grilled cuttlefish and *senyoret* paella (made with squid and monkfish). The outpost also offers sun loungers, where sandwiches can be enjoyed in true Spanish style – on the sand.
laplayademoda.com

Salvador Barrés had dreamt of opening a bar dedicated to oysters since the 1990s but it wasn't until 2015 that he, along with co-founder Antonio Ladrillo, made his dream a reality. It was worth the wait: everything from the industrial interiors to the wine list and the fare itself, has been painstakingly thought through. "When you have a simple business model, it is important to keep it that way," says Ladrillo. Oysters are the star of the show but the rest of the menu more than keeps up – highlights include the Galician sea urchin and *gildas* (olive and anchovy skewers). "We know that whoever enters Ostras Pedrín will end up coming back," says Barrés.
ostraspedrin.es

DRINKING & DINING

RESTAURANT
SALZILLO
Murcia, Murcia

Spain is famous for its gastronomy and produce but no region is as highly-regarded, or undiscovered, as Murcia. Known as Europe's Orchard, the area's location provides the perfect conditions for growing fruit, vegetables and pulses, while its proximity to the coast also affords a wealth of quality seafood. Salzillo, a family-run restaurant that opened in 1988, is a master at handling the region's bounty. The Murcian institution serves a creative menu of Spanish classics with a modern twist. Don't skip on wine: Salzillo has an impressive selection of local bottles.
restaurantesalzillo.com

RESTAURANT
NOOR
Córdoba, Andalucía

Paco Morales's Noor explores the cuisine of Al-Ándalus, the historical name for the Iberian peninsula when it was under Muslim rule. The two-Michelin-starred chef opened the restaurant in 2016 and, along with a team of historians and designers, has developed a gastronomic experience that takes diners on a theatrical journey through Córdoba's past. Everything has been meticulously thought through, from the restaurant's name (which means 'light' in Arabic) to the interior, which is peppered with Moorish influences. But it's not all smoke and mirrors: Morales has managed to elevate medieval fare for a modern audience – with flair.
noorrestaurant.es

RESTAURANT
LAS TERESAS
Seville

With chunky legs of *jamón* swinging above the bar, tables spilling out onto the street and tiled walls covered with posters of bullfighters and flamenco dancers, it doesn't get much more Seville than this. Founded in 1870, Las Teresas has been run by the same family since 1920. Its location in the heart of the buzzing Santa Cruz neighbourhood means that the bar is perennially packed, but the patrons are as likely to be locals knocking back a *caña* as tourists looking for a slice of authentic Spain. It's worth braving the crowds for the paper-thin *jamón ibérico de bellota*, which melts on the tongue.
lasteresas.es

DRINKING & DINING

RESTAURANTS · DISCOVER SPAIN

RESTAURANT
EL CUARTEL DEL MAR
Chiclana de la Frontera, Andalucía

Named for the military police quarters it once housed, El Cuartel del Mar provides sweeping views over Barrosa beach from its roof terrace. "Respect for the environment was of the utmost importance in the project," says lead architect Paula Rosales. "Both from the perspective of nature – this is a key bird-watching location – and also considering the building's history." Depending on the season, *atún de almadraba* (blue-fin tuna) can be found on the menu. It is caught offshore using traditional methods that trap the fish in nets as they migrate from the Atlantic to the Mediterranean. *elcuarteldelmar.com*

SPAIN

RESTAURANT
EL PIMPI
Málaga

El Pimpi is a Málaga institution. Founded in 1971 by Paco Campos and Pepe Cobos, this warren of rooms set across an 18th-century townhouse includes a traditional tavern, a tapas bar and an outdoor terrace with views of the city's Roman theatre. The emblematic *Salón de los Barriles* would once have been used to store locally-produced moscatel wine but is today stacked with barrels bearing chalk-scrawled messages from illustrious past diners. The restaurant serves classic Malagueño dishes – using organic produce from its garden – such as *ensalada Malagueña* with potato, orange and baked cod. It also hosts regular flamenco performances.
elpimpi.com

DRINKING & DINING

RESTAURANT
LA COSMO
Málaga

Fare trade
The Málaga region has a long history of food production and trade: the Phoenicians founded the port in 1000BC and it is widely believed that they named the city Malaka after their word for salt.

Steps away from Málaga's Alcazaba fort is homegrown talent Dani Carnero's most contemporary bistro. As with his other two restaurants, La Cosmo has a clear Andalucian influence but here the chef takes a simpler approach – he can often be seen cooking oysters over flames in the open kitchen. "It's about presenting a quality product with *pellizco*," he says, borrowing a flamenco term to describe his search for authenticity. His efforts to keep the region's gastronomic memory alive can be savoured in his grilled sardines in *escabeche*, a traditional paprika brine used for preserving food.
lacosmo.es

SPAIN

RESTAURANT
LHARDY
Madrid

Lhardy, one of Madrid's oldest restaurants, was rumoured to have been a favourite of Queen Isabella II, who would arrive from the nearby palace in disguise with her maids in tow. Since its founding in 1839 by Emilio Huguenin Lhardy, its gilded salons have also hosted the city's most influential politicians, writers and artists. A restoration by its Galician owners Pescaderías Coruñesas, who rescued it from closure in 2021, has updated the institution without sacrificing its old-school charm. During the colder months, stop in for broth from the samovar, a tradition which dates from 1885.
lhardy.com

RESTAURANT
LA PARRA
Madrid

This third-generation-owned restaurant has been like a home, not only to Madrid's high society but also to sisters Andrea and Tessa Sánchez Walmsley who took over the British-Andalucian outpost from their parents. "We went to school down the road and would eat lunch here every day with all the actors and aristocrats," says Andrea, explaining the familial warmth that has kept patrons coming back for 40 years. The menu contains classics such as roast beef and *cochinillo* (suckling pig).
restaurante-laparra.com

RESTAURANT
JOSEFITA
Madrid

Sometimes, in an effort to move into the future, a detour into the past is necessary. Sol Perez-Fragero navigated that tricky dance when opening bistro Josefita. The vibrant bar was named after her grandmother's nickname for her and offers an interior filled with refined vintage textures and patterns – an homage to her grandparents' home near Córdoba. Another link to her childhood, Perez-Fragero uses the local butcher from her hometown for several items on the menu. Andalucian family recipes such as *albondigas de pescado* (fish balls) are served alongside dishes from across the peninsula.
josefitabar.es

RESTAURANT
GANBARA
San Sebastián

The Basque Country is the home of the *pintxo*, meaning "spike" in Basque. These small bites, often served on bread held together with a skewer or toothpick, are a regional delicacy. One of the best places to sample them is at Ganbara, a San Sebastián institution which opened in the city's old town in 1984. It was one of the first *pintxo* spots to open following the launch of the Basque culinary movement, which was led by local chefs who popularised the miniature meals. Ganbara is now run by brother and sister duo Nagore and Amaiur Martínez and menu highlights include the spider crab tartlet and sautéed mushrooms with egg yolk.
ganbarajatetxea.com

RESTAURANT
REKONDO
San Sebastián

Rekondo is known for having one of the best wine lists in the world, and certainly in Spain. Diners and wine enthusiasts are in good hands with the collection of more than 100,000 bottles in Txomin Rekondo's expansive cellar. Rekondo opened his namesake restaurant in 1964 after inheriting his family's farmhouse at the base of Monte Igueldo in San Sebastián. It offers classic Basque dishes made with high-quality ingredients served on its leafy terrace with views of the bay.
rekondo.com

DRINKING & DINING

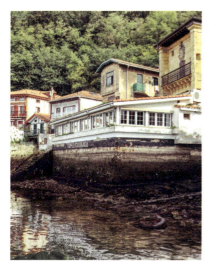

RESTAURANT
CASA CÁMARA
Pasai Donibane, Basque Country

Casa Cámara has been serving first-rate seafood to the people of Pasai Donibane, a small fishing community 30-minutes drive from San Sebastián, since 1884. The building, which is perched on the harbourfront, was once a warehouse where *arrantzales* (fishermen) would unload their catch before it was sold at market. Original owner Pablo Cámara converted the space into a seafront restaurant. Four generations later, it has not lost its magic: although the interior has been updated, the harbour views remain unmatched and the dishes are as fresh as ever.
casacamara.com

Take your pick
The restaurant is famous for its fresh lobster and crab – in fact, diners can hand-select their crustacean from a trap that's lifted directly from the water into the centre of the restaurant with a rope and pulley.

RESTAURANT
GURE TOKI
Bilbao

Tucked away in the corner of the Plaza Nueva in Bilbao's old quarter, Gure Toki is a rare example of an established restaurant that has developed modern flair. Originally opened in 1982 as a traditional *taberna* (bar) serving sharing portions of patatas bravas, the second generation of owners took over and reimagined the space as a contemporary take on Basque cuisine. Today the joint caters to a younger crowd, and you can find siblings Ivan and Begoña Siles in the kitchen while Yolanda serves new-wave *pintxos* (as well as the old classics) with pride.
guretoki.com

RESTAURANT
BASCOOK
Bilbao

Bascook chef and owner Aitor Elizegi has been serving his own menu of Basque dishes with a Japanese twist since 2010. Located in a former salt warehouse that sat neglected, the restaurant's dining area is low-lit and atmospheric, with bare stone walls and a comfortable hum of happy diners within. Elizegi himself is known throughout the region for his creative culinary offering – the Bilbao local is also the owner of nearby Txocook, which focuses on traditional Basque fare. Opt for the stuffed maki or Iberian pork.
bascook.com

DRINKING & DINING

RESTAURANT
CASA MARCIAL
Arriondas, Asturias

In a bucolic village 10km from the Asturian coast you'll find Casa Marcial. The property has been in the hands of Nacho Manzano's family for generations; he was born upstairs. The world-class restaurant serves classic Asturian comfort food such as *tortas de maíz* (corn fritters). Despite its two Michelin stars, Casa Marcial is still a welcoming, family affair – Manzano's sister, Sandra, is the maître-d'. "Asturian food culture is rustic, like an old man with lots of personality," says Manzano. "Our mothers and grandmothers probably played a part in nursing our healthy appetites too."
casamarcial.es

SPAIN

RESTAURANT
LA CASETA DE BOMBAS
Santander

From Santander-based hospitality group Deluz y Compañía comes La Caseta de Bombas, set in the old pump house of the city's former dry dock. Sandwiched between Santander bay and the concert hall, the restaurant sits on the water's edge with striking views. Every detail has been considered by owners and siblings Lucía and Carlos Zamora (*see page 85*), who source ingredients from small-scale producers, including seafood from the fish market and cheese from a family-run organic farm. Diners can also expect impeccable service – each waiter will be able to tell you the provenance of every ingredient on the menu.
lacasetadebombas.es

RESTAURANT
BAR DO PORTO
Corrubedo, Galicia

Regional ally
Bar do Porto aims to support the local community: the bar's bread comes from family-run bakery Sieira Charlin while razor clams and other fish are sourced from the area's specialist seafood shops.

In Corrubedo, British architect David Chipperfield has reimagined Bar do Porto, a local spot that had been closed for more than 30 years. Chipperfield recognised the quality of the region's food as well as something ineffable beyond it. The bar reopened in 2020, picking up where it had left off as a place where villagers can connect over a quick drink and a hearty meal. For the interior, Chipperfield collaborated with Galician architect Sofia Blanco Santos to help ensure the spirit of the venue would stay true to the original – down to old sports trophies that were left by the previous owners.
+34 981 865 370

RESTAURANT
ES XARCU
Ibiza

Hidden among the pine trees on an unspoilt Ibiza beach is Es Xarcu, a restaurant that's been open since the 1980s. The shoreside spot is run by Caridad Cabañero and her husband Mariano Torres who, along with help from their family members, have built a reputation for serving some of the island's best seafood – and in one of its best locations. The refined Mediterranean menu, singular setting and exceptional service (Cabañero knows her long-time customers' table preferences by heart) have put Es Xarcu firmly on the map.
esxarcurestaurante.com

DRINKING & DINING

RESTAURANT
EL CAMINO
Mallorca

Having redefined Spanish cuisine in the British capital with the chain of Barrafina restaurants, English restaurateur Eddie Hart set out on a much bigger challenge: serving tapas in Spain. His restaurant El Camino sits at the centre of Palma's old town, just steps away from the 13th-century cathedral. The menu by Mallorquín chef Cristian Rivera includes classics such as Trempó salad, creamy *croquetas* and scallops with garlic. The smart interior was designed by local interior design studio Elsa Oliveras and features one long marble-topped bar with brushed bronze lights hanging above each place setting.
elcaminopalma.es

RESTAURANT
ULISSES
Menorca

In the midst of Ciutadella's bustling fish market is a seafood restaurant with a focus on Menorquín fare. Local Joan Canals opened the joint in 2012 with the aim of elevating the island's produce and cuisine. Canals hails from a traditional fishing family, so it's no surprise that most of the menu is seafood-based – in fact, most of what ends up on plates is caught by the restaurant's two fishing boats. The inventive menu changes daily (according to what's available at sea and market), with Canals keen to add his own twist: dishes include tempura monkfish and baked fish with *sobrasada* (spicy sausage).
ulissesbar.com

BAKERY
THE LOAF
San Sebastián

Bread plays an important role in Basque cuisine, though normally in the form of a baguette. In 2013 a group of bakers went against the grain and launched The Loaf in San Sebastián's Gros neighbourhood, which sells everything from sourdough to speciality coffee. The café-bakery has since grown to include four outposts around the city; the original location next to Zurriola beach has remained the favourite spot for coffee and brunch. If the smell of freshly-baked bread doesn't draw you in, the atmosphere will: pared-back furnishings create a casual and welcoming interior while large windows look out onto the incoming waves.
theloaf.eus

BAKERY
CLOUDSTREET BAKERY
Barcelona

When Mexico-born Ton Cortés arrived in Barcelona as a music student, he took up baking to finance his studies. The passion soon took hold and in 2013 he launched Cloudstreet Bakery, which occupies a site that has been a bakery for over a century. Cortés creates a mix of Catalan classics including *coca de forner* flatbreads and seasonal Mexican specialities such as the sweet *pan de muertos*. "We've created a family-like bond with our customers," says Manel Benazet, who runs Cloudstreet alongside Cortés and his sister Zitaima. "They trust in our abilities to create quality artisan products using organic ingredients."
cloudstreet.es

DRINKING & DINING

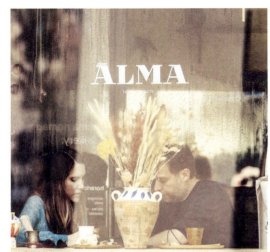

BAKERY
ALMA NOMAD
Madrid

Alma Nomad's founders Timi Árgyélán and Joaquín Escrivá never expected that transplanting the bakery from its original location in Árgyélán's native Hungary to Madrid's leafy Plaza de Olavide neighbourhood would be such a success. "Madrileños have a serious sweet tooth," says Escrivá, explaining the queue which often extends well beyond the front door. Large windows allow waiting customers to peruse the oven-fresh spoils, from chocolate croissants and ricotta and blood-orange puff pastry tarts to brioche-like challah bread.
+34 613 026 888

SWEET TREATS
LA DUQUESITA
Madrid

Along with its delectable pastries, La Duquesita serves up a slice of Madrid's history. Founded in 1914, the bakery was rescued from closure in 2015 by a team that included one of Spain's best-known pastry and dessert chefs, Oriol Balaguer. Though recognised for his innovative techniques (he spent seven years at El Bulli under Ferran Adrià), Balaguer has created a selection of treats for the bakery that are artisanal, traditional and of top quality. In 2021 the confectionery expanded into the retail space next door with its very own tea room, designed to serve as a sort of *terraza* where patrons can linger over their Tarta Duquesita while sipping champagne.
laduquesita.es

SWEET TREATS
VACHATA
Valencia

Horchata is a milky Valencian delicacy made from tiger nuts that's mixed with sugar and served ice cold with a side of fartons, a sweet pastry traditionally dunked into the drink. Marta Planells (*pictured*) opened a contemporary take on the humble *horchatería* in the city's Ruzafa neighbourhood in 2020, where she sells her homemade iteration. The entrepreneur is far from a newcomer. In fact, Planells hails from a family of renowned *horchata* makers – her grandfather even sold its machinery in the 1940s. "I wanted to follow the family tradition but with a modern approach," she says.
+34 640 175 342

SWEET TREATS
HELADERÍA CA'N MIQUEL
Mallorca

This ice-cream institution, founded in 1979, claims to be the first parlour in Spain to offer a selection of savoury flavours. Heladería Ca'n Miquel is now run by the second and third-generation owners but it continues to honour the more than 150 recipes created by founder Miquel Solivellas. Its experimental flavours include everything from avocado to roquefort. But those with a sweet tooth won't be disappointed: sorbets are made with apricots, strawberries and lemons from a local agricultural cooperative, and are free from colourings and preservatives. *heladeriacanmiquel.com*

CAFÉ
GRAN CAFÉ SANTANDER
Madrid

Madrid's Plaza de Santa Bárbara is lined with architectural gems from the turn of the 20th century including this café-restaurant which has been given a new lease of life. The original spot was run by the same family for more than 50 years before it closed in 2019. When Paco Quirós and Carlos Crespo of Grupo Cañadío took over they enlisted the help of interior designer Sandra Tarruella. Today, it is an homage to the grand European cafés of yore with olive-green tiles and a walnut-topped bar. As well as speciality coffee, the menu features Cantabrian dishes such as *croquetas* and a sublimely soft *tortilla de patatas*.
grancafesantander.com

CAFÉ
CAFÉ BAR EL MUELLE
Santiago de Compostela, Galicia

Café Bar el Muelle became a favourite haunt of Galician writers and intellectuals throughout the 1930s. In fact, some punters have been coming for as long as 50 years for their morning coffee, which is served in the iconic blue-and-white cups made by local porcelain company Sargadelos (*see page 93*). After a stint as a DJ in Berlin, owner Pablo Iglesias returned to take over the business from his parents and has since added a DJ booth and opened an online record shop. The interior maintains an old-school feel, with pink heart-shaped Formica chairs that famously caught the eye of film director Pedro Almodóvar when he visited. *elmuelle1931.com*

CAFÉ
CAFÉ IRUÑA
Pamplona, Navarre

For anyone who has read Ernest Hemingway's *The Sun Also Rises*, Café Iruña will evoke images of hazy summer days drinking absinthe on the terrace in Pamplona's Plaza del Castillo. While you won't find absinthe on the menu anymore, the café has remained largely unchanged since the author's many visits in the 1920s. Ornate pillars, marble-topped tables and original bentwood chairs still fill the interior today. Diners can even share a *caña* with the famed author in Hemingway's corner, where a gilded life-size statue can be found casually resting against the bar. *cafeiruna.com*

SPAIN

SPECIALITY COFFEE
NOMAD COFFEE
Barcelona

Jordi Mestre (*pictured, bottom on left*) launched Nomad in 2011 as a portable coffee cart that travelled around London's street markets. Three years later he returned to his native Barcelona where he founded his own speciality roastery and coffee shop – one of the first of its kind in the Spanish city. It has since grown to encompass a second café as well as offering workshops and a home-delivery subscription service. "We source some of the world's best and rarest coffees and work with some really amazing producers," says Mestre. "We're a team who love what we do and I believe you can taste that in our coffees."
nomadcoffee.es

SPECIALITY COFFEE
TOMA CAFÉ
Madrid

"I found that the coffee here was making me sick," says Argentina-born Santiago Rigoni of his initial experience with Spanish coffee. The culprit? *Torrefacto*, a commercial method of sugar-roasting coffee beans. Though he and partner Patricia Alda (*both pictured*) were working in marketing, they became obsessed with bringing better coffee to Madrid and in 2011 they opened Toma Café. The cult following they developed led them to launch Toma Café 2 in 2017, where patrons can enjoy small bites along with coffee made from beans they roast just a few streets away. "Feeding the *barrio* economy this way creates real sustainability," says Rigoni.
toma.cafe

SPECIALITY COFFEE
OHBABA
San Sebastián

There are countless cafés in Spain that serve a basic *café con leche* but change is being spearheaded by speciality coffee shops such as Ohbaba, which was founded in 2020 by Nora Esnaola and her partner Koldo Amondarain. Esnaola saw an opportunity in San Sebastián for a modern café and opened the first plant-based coffee shop in northern Spain. Ohbaba is growing a healthy customer base of young locals and visitors, although Esnaola admits take up is slow: "It takes a lot of time for people to change their ways but we're here for the long haul."
ohbabakofi.com

SPECIALITY COFFEE
LA MOLIENDA
Mallorca

Cousins Miquel Calvente and Toni Emazabel (*both pictured, Calvente on left, Emazabel on right*) founded La Molienda in their hometown of Palma in 2013 after working in the competitive London café scene. The pair realised that many Spanish cafeterias paid little attention to the quality and provenance of their coffee and so they set out to change this. The small venue opened on Carrer de les Caputxines in 2013 and was the first speciality café in Mallorca – it now counts three outposts in the city. The team roasts its own beans, which are sourced from small producers in Central America and Africa. La Molienda also distributes its coffee to other businesses on the island.
lamolienda.es

WINERY
GÓMEZ CRUZADO
Haro, La Rioja

La Rioja is Spain's most famous wine-producing region, with some 500 wineries across 54,000 hectares in the province. One such winery is Gómez Cruzado, which was established in 1886. Today, this small winery is owned by the Baños Carrera family, who purchased the property in the early 2000s to help bring its wine-making facilities up to date. Vintner David González (*pictured*) has overseen the production since 2013 and has created a superior selection of terroir-driven wines. Highlights include Honorable – made from Tempranillo (the principal grape of Rioja wine) grown at higher elevations – and Pancrudo, a red made from Grenache.
gomezcruzado.com

WINERY
BÀRBARA FORÉS
Tarragona, Cataluña

Now in its sixth generation, Bàrbara Forés is a small and influential family-run winery in Cataluña's Terra Alta area. The business is headed by mother-and-daughter duo Carmen and Pili Sanmartín Ferrer (with help from Carmen's husband Manolo), who pride themselves on their organic and traditional methods – from hand-picking grapes to skin-contact maceration. These techniques are largely unchanged since the winery was founded (by the son of Bàrbara Forés) in the late 19th-century. The cellar is known for its exceptional white wines made from the Garnatxa Blanca grape.
cellerbarbarafores.com

DRINKING & DINING

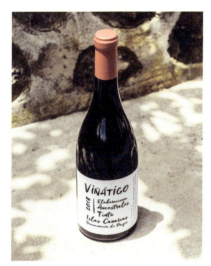

WINERY
BODEGAS VIÑÁTIGO
Tenerife

Jorge Méndez Díaz (*pictured*) is carrying on a wine-making tradition that goes back five generations – his family has cultivated 13 of Tenerife's native grapes. "In the 1980s, many people began introducing foreign grape varieties but we strove to maintain the essence of the island's own," he says. "We have vines grown from those planted by my great-grandfather that will live for at least another 200 years." The winery's ancestral reds are made using traditional techniques such as grape-treading and visitors can sample them inside a cylindrical building made from volcanic rock.
bodegasvinatigo.com

SPAIN

BAR
EL RINCONCILLO
Seville

Seville's oldest bar, founded in 1670, is showing its age in the best way possible. The De Rueda family, who have run this enduring favourite since 1858, have preserved original details including carved-wood vitrines that rise up to the double-height ceiling. A mahogany bar extends through the space, presenting more than a mere spot to rest one's drink, as waiters still use the varnished surface for writing each patron's order in chalk. Pair a glass of wine from the mountains north of the city with *carrilladas de cerdo* (pork-cheek stew) for a winning combination.
elrinconcillo.es

DRINKING & DINING

BAR
DANI BRASSERIE
Madrid

Occupying the coveted rooftop spot of Madrid's Four Seasons hotel is Dani Brasserie, led by fêted Spanish chef Dani García. The pretty (and often packed) rooftop bar and restaurant opened in 2020 to the delight of Madrileños with its leafy, light-filled interior and sun-drenched terrace. The brasserie serves everything from breakfast to indulgent dinners with a menu designed by the three-Michelin-starred chef. It's in the evening though, as the sun sets across the city and the inventive cocktails (inspired by Spain and each of its regions) start to flow, that this space truly comes into its own.
danibrasserie.com

BAR
GOTA
Madrid

BAR
SAVAS
Madrid

Gintas Arlauskas and Dovile Krauzaite (*both pictured*) left Lithuania in 2008 with the intention of staying in Madrid for just one month. Then they began working at pioneering restaurant Sudestada, which was responsible for bringing Asian fusion to Spain, and that changed everything. In 2019 the pair opened Savas, an intimate cocktail bar with a pared-back interior reminiscent of a homely kitchen – albeit a very nice one. "Back home, secrets were told in the kitchen – it's such a big part of us," says Krauzante. Don't miss the Polsky Fizz, which has a base of bison-grass vodka and apple juice.
Calle de la Sombrerería 3

Fede Graciano started his natural wine bar in the back room of his café – "It was like a laboratory," he says. Less than a year later, Graciano decided to move the bar into its own space. The interiors, a brutalist-inspired collaboration between Danish design studio Frama and Madrid's Plantea Estudio, create a vibe that is both cosy and futuristic. Carefully selected wines pair nicely with the kitchen's rotating four-week menu while staff spin records on the bar's turntables. Following an evening at this lively bar, patrons can put a well-needed pep in their step at Graciano's initial venture, Acid café.
gotawine.es

DRINKING & DINING

BAR
BAR COCK
Madrid

Its stained-glass windows, wood-panelled walls and ornate fireplace may fool you into thinking you've stepped into an aristocratic country home but Bar Cock is just steps from the main thoroughfare of Gran Vía. The Madrid institution opened in 1921 – and famously managed to keep pouring drinks even throughout the Civil War – soon becoming a firm favourite among the city's creatives. The bar remains the hangout of choice for Madrid's editors and journalists and was reputedly Francis Bacon's go-to drinking hole in the city.
+34 915 322 826

BAR
BALIUS
Barcelona

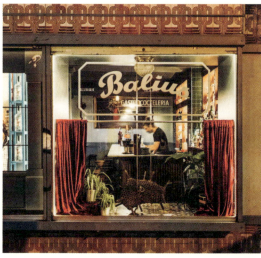

This vermut and cocktail bar was once a pharmacy that went by the same name. The exterior is recognisable by its retro *modernisme*-era tiles and inside the red banquettes and low light create a moody speakeasy-like atmposphere. A variety of vermut supplements a lengthy list of craft cocktails (we recommend the "sambac" made with pisco, jasmine, chamomile and citrus). The food offering is eclectic and minimal: think Cantabrian anchovies, *fuets* (sausage) and salmon cubes marinated in soy vinaigrette and honey.
baliusbar.com

BAR
GRAN MARTÍNEZ
Valencia

With grand chequerboard floors, wood panelling and dim lighting, Valencia's Gran Martínez cocktail bar feels as if it has been plucked from another time. The former pharmacy was built in the 19th century by a certain Señor Martínez (hence the name) and its storied history is apparent in the apothecary shelving lining the walls. The sophisticated spot is once again known for its concoctions – only now they are the work of cocktail master Pedro Araujo. The menu lists everything from much-loved classics to experimental tipples, served with a side of Michelin-starred snacks and live music.
granmartinez.com

BREWERY
ESTRELLA GALICIA
A Coruña, Galicia

The crisp golden lager of Estrella Galicia can be found across Spain but its flavour is said to be superior when enjoyed in the seaside city of A Coruña where it was born. Production of the beer has exploded since the family-run business was founded in 1906 – it now produces an average of 200m litres every year. Beer enthusiasts can tour the brewery or visit the *cervecería* in the city's Cuatro Caminos neighbourhood: a wood-panelled beer hall which opened in 1925 and serves special brews including unpasteurised beer from the bodega and experimental seasonal blends that you'd be hard pushed to find anywhere else.
estrellagalicia.es

CIDER PRODUCER
ASTARBE SAGARDOTEGIA
Astigarraga, Basque Country

Joseba Astarbe's family has been making cider since the 16th century in Astigarraga. The town is known as the birthplace of Basque cider, which was historically drunk by seamen to ward off scurvy. The cidery is run by siblings Joseba, Hur (*both pictured, Joseba on left*) and Kizkitza, who work "the old way" – they grow trees from wild seeds and ferment juice in chestnut barrels. During *txotx* season (named after the wooden plug on the side of a barrel) visitors are invited to fill their glasses straight from the source.
astarbe.eus

SPAIN

MARKET
MERCADO DE VALLEHERMOSO
Madrid

To put a finger on the pulse of a *barrio* and its people, visit the *mercado municipal*. Spanish markets sell fresh food direct from suppliers and act as indoor *plazas* where neighbours can socialise while they shop. While many across the country have been threatened by supermarket chains, Madrid's Mercado Vallehermoso, which was founded in 1931, has weathered economic ups and downs to serve as a model for how markets can preserve traditions while innovating at the same time. In 2015, when only a third of the stalls were occupied, the market welcomed a fresh face that shifted its fortunes – Kitchen 154. The Asian-street-food-inspired stand brought major increases in footfall. Today, back at full occupancy, the *mercado* is home to more than 50 stalls which range from classic fruit and vegetable vendors to speciality coffee stands.

DRINKING & DINING

MARKET
MERCADO CENTRAL DE VALENCIA
Valencia

Valencians are a lucky bunch: the city hosts more than 15 food markets – the largest and most well-known being the Mercado Central de Valencia. A Heritage of Cultural Interest site, the structure is an architectural feat in steel and glass which opened in 1928. Inside, some 1,200 retailers sell everything from fruit to seafood (look out for the live eels) and local delicacies. Once you've haggled for *jamón* and finished a glass of *horchata*, head to Central Bar, a tapas restaurant run by Michelin-starred chef Ricard Camarena.

MARKET
MERCADO DE LA ESPERANZA
Santander

As a nation, Spain consumes more seafood than any other European country – and Santander may well be the nucleus of the phenomenon. The Mercado de la Esperanza, which translates as "Market of Hope", is stacked with all manner of gills, fins and scales as well as other produce. The space was built in 1904 as part of a wave of new projects across Spain that emulated the iron-and-glass Les Halles Centrales in Paris (which was controversially demolished in the 1970s). Thankfully, Santander's main *mercado* remains largely unaltered and is frequented by everyone from pensioners and students to distinguished chefs.

DRINKING & DINING

MARKET
ERRIBERA MERKATUA
Bilbao

This stately market on the Río Nervión is the largest covered market in Europe and the buzzing centre of Bilbao's medieval quarter, the Casco Viejo neighbourhood. The art deco building was finished in 1929 to replace its open air predecessor and is the creation of architect Pedro Ispizua (who trained alongside Gaudí). The market spans three floors with areas dedicated to seafood, meats and cheeses, fruit and vegetables, and a gourmet street-food court for a well-earned post-market meal. Stop by Amua by Zarate for fresh seafood or La Bodeguilla for an endless, and tasty, selection of *pintxos*.

Fresh pickings
La Ribera is a restaurant and jazz bar located at the front of the building. Pop in after a day at the market and the chef will cook a meal with your new ingredients for only €8.

The Spanish are masters when it come to food and drink – San Sebastián has the world's highest concentration of Michelin-starred restaurants and tapas is a global hit. We meet three entrepreneurs in the business.

MEET THE EXPERTS

CHEESE SHOP OWNER
CLARA DIEZ
Formaje

Self-proclaimed cheese activist Clara Diez founded her Madrid-based shop with her husband Adrián to change the narrative around cheese.

Tell us a little about the inspiration behind Formaje.
After working in the artisanal cheese sector for about eight years, we realised that the public had a dated perception of the cheese world. We decided that it would be interesting to create a platform where the product could be sold, exhibited and communicated in a more modern manner. Formaje takes inspiration from different fields: fashion, architecture and interior design, helping create a renewed discourse around cheese.

What is your favourite Spanish cheese and why?
Queixo do País, a traditional Galician cheese made by an elderly woman named Josefa and her young team. It is a raw milk product, matured for only 20 or 30 days, which was traditionally made by women in their homes with the milk from the family cows.

How is the food scene in Madrid evolving?
Rapidly. A number of truly groundbreaking new businesses have opened, mixing the best of Spanish culture with more international references. I love how they are managing to preserve the traditional essence of the city while presenting something new.

DRINKING & DINING

RESTAURATEUR
CARLOS ZAMORA
Deluz y Compañía

FOOD RETAILERS
NATALIA & IRENE ESTELLÉS PALANCA
Palanca Carnissers

Following a successful career in the hospitality industry, Carlos Zamora joined forces with his sister Lucía Zamora to start restaurant company Deluz y Compañía.

Sisters Natalia and Irene Estellés Palanca are the current owners of family butchers Palanca Carnissers, which operates out of the Mercado Central de Valencia.

How did Deluz y Compañía begin?
I was born in Santander but spent many years overseas and in other parts of Spain working in hospitality management and consulting. In 2006 I returned to Santander and my sister and I decided we wanted to open a restaurant in our grandparents' old home and call it Deluz. Eventually we created Deluz y Compañía, which combined our passions – mine for opening restaurants and hers for positive social impact. From the start, we were connecting with small suppliers and treating and paying our workers fairly.

Why is it important to you to share a love of food?
We try to create an atmosphere where everyone feels at home. Where you have lived, what you've eaten – that makes you who you are, and we wanted to share that.

What makes a good restaurant?
There are the obvious things such as location, the ambience, the atmosphere and the architectural elements that make people want to stay and also to come back. But you also need to first look at the *barrio*, since your main income will always be the base of people who live near you. People also come back if they get treated well, and word of mouth has more power than any social media campaign.

How did the business start?
Our great grandparents started Palanca Carnissers in 1914 and it has been run by four generations since. The current site has been in operation since the Mercado Central de Valencia opened in 1928 and each generation has added something new.

How have you adapted the business for a modern clientele?
We have introduced more contemporary branding to appeal to a younger customer, enlisting the help of graphic designer Vicente Luján to reimagine the stall. We also brought in new products and we've adapted our approach to the butchery too: we now sell specialist meats such as dry aged Spanish beef and we have also introduced an online ordering system. We still sell our traditional family recipes that have been passed down through the years though.

How has the purchase of food in Spain changed?
The influx of modern supermarkets has forced us to be flexible – our customers are looking for the best quality, spanning the products we sell to the presentation, service and expertise we provide.

What advice would you give to someone taking over a family business?
There is a great deal of passion that has been poured into the business by past generations – you cannot forget the effort they have gone to to make the company a success. But it must also work for you.

This nation of makers knows a thing or two about retail and has plenty to offer whether you're in the market for a leather handbag, a handwoven blanket or even a cape. Our advice? Pack an empty suitcase.

DESIGN & RETAIL

From carpenters to weavers, leatherworkers to jewellers, Spain is a country of makers with a long history of world-leading artisanship. It's little wonder then, that many leading international brands still choose to have their wares produced in the country. That's not to say that the Spanish are only manufacturing for others. Homegrown brands such as lighting company Santa & Cole and ceramics-maker Sargadelos have long been combining contemporary forms with mid-century flair to produce some of the most sought-after design objects. A whole host of new labels are also securing their position on the fashion industry's world stage. All this comes together to make Spain's cities true retail hubs: high streets tend to be far less chain-heavy than other European centres, aside from national stalwarts El Corte Inglés and Inditex – the Galicia-based parent company behind fashion behemoth Zara. It's time to go shopping.

THE EDIT

1 Textiles
Colourful rugs, mohair shawls and blankets woven in an old monastery – these are the fabric brands to know.

2 Lighting
The Cataluña institution that's still shining bright.

3 Ceramics
A duo in Valencia turning out contemporary pieces and an iconic Galician brand.

4 Specialist shops
From fans to flowers – you name it, we've found it. Here are the shops that do one thing incredibly well.

5 Concept stores
Two shops that have turned retail into an artform.

6 Fashion
The brands that offer a laidback, sunny and distinctly Spanish look.

7 Shoes
Leather sandals, espadrilles, loafers and more.

8 The experts
A designer, retailer and manufacturer spill the beans on the current design and retail scene in Spain.

DESIGN & RETAIL

TEXTILES
NANIMARQUINA
Barcelona

"Barcelona is a city that breathes creativity and has long been a pioneer of Spanish design," says Nani Marquina. She launched her eponymous textiles brand in 1987 after spotting a gap in the market for colourful contemporary rug designs. Today Marquina works with skilled artisans in India, Pakistan and Nepal to produce pieces that combine her design nous with ancient weaving techniques. She has also produced collaborations with an array of Spanish creatives, from Jaime Hayon (*see page 112*) to Catalan painter Claudia Valsells.
nanimarquina.com

SPAIN

TEXTILES
MANTAS EZCARAY
Ezcaray, La Rioja

Based in a picturesque village in the northern region of La Rioja, Mantas Ezcaray started in the 1930s when Cecilio Valgañón decided that, instead of cloths, he would adapt his handlooms to manufacture scarves, shawls and blankets. He incorporated mohair from local Angora goats and today the firm has garnered international acclaim for its quality and dedication to age-old techniques that have largely vanished. The workshop – now run by Valgañón's grandchildren – is the beating heart of the company, where the wools and fibres are washed, brushed, dyed and woven entirely by hand.
mantasezcaray.com

Softly does it
Mohair is known as one of the most luxurious fibres for its warmth, shine and softness – but also for needing constant care.

TEXTILES
ÁBBATTE
Segovia, Castilla y León

Among the ruins of a 13th-century monastery you'll find textiles brand Ábbatte, known for its all-natural handwoven blankets, cushions and wallhangings. Former biologist Elena Goded Rambaud and designer Camilla Lanzas Goded (*both pictured, Elena on right*) launched the company in 2012 with the aim of reviving the area's textile traditions. The mother and daughter duo produce products woven by specialists at the Segovia headquarters, which has been transformed from a derelict abbey. Today, it includes a shop, studios and botanical garden where Elena grows plants for unique dyes. *abbatte.com*

LIGHTING
SANTA & COLE
Barcelona

Catalan lighting brand Santa & Cole was founded in the mid-1980s by Javier Nieto Santa, Gabriel Ordeig Cole and Nina Masó. Their goal was simple: to reintroduce iconic discontinued products to a new generation. They began by convincing designer Miguel Milá to let them bring his TMM floor lamp (which remains a bestseller) back into production and have since added designs from mid-century masters including André Ricard and Ilmari Tapiovaara. Today, a team also develops new designs and often enlists the help of big-name contemporary talent such as Antoni Arola and Anthony Dickens. *santacole.com*

Back to school
Santa & Cole's HQ is located in the former Parc de Belloch primary school in the Cataluña countryside. Acquired in 2003, it has been repurposed as a playground for learning and experimentation.

CERAMICS
CANOA LAB
Valencia

Canoa Lab's handcrafted ceramics are an antithesis to mass-produced tableware. Husband-and-wife duo Pedro Paz and Raquel Vidal (*both pictured*) launched the studio in Valencia in 2016. "There is a ceramic tradition that exists in this city and its surroundings," says Paz. The pair create their designs from local stoneware, followed by multiple layers of self-formulated glazes. "We take a lot of inspiration from ancient culture and techniques – especially primitive designs, which are produced with as few tools as possible," Paz explains. The result is an elegant ceramic that is truly one of a kind.
canoalab.com

DESIGN & RETAIL

CERAMICS
SARGADELOS
Cervo, Galicia

The story of this highly regarded ceramics company with its distinctive blue-and-white patterns inspired by Galician and Celtic motifs dates back to the early 1800s. Sargadelos was given fresh impetus when the firm built the current circular production building and cultural centre in 1968 with the aim to revive and preserve traditional Galician arts. Today, some 200 workers produce close to half a million pieces of hand-painted porcelain every year, from classic dinner sets and coffee cups to more whimsical carnival masks and even beer taps for Estrella Galicia (*see page 78*).
sargadelos.com

SPECIALIST SHOP
ARQUINESIA
Mallorca

Arquinesia – combining the words archipelago and Gymnesia (the ancient name of the Balearic Islands) – is a perfume brand inspired by its surroundings. Its elegant store, hidden on a cobbled side street in Palma's historic centre, is set in a townhouse with tiled floors, beamed ceilings and antique cabinets containing fragrances such as Orange, Fig, Sea Breeze and Secret Garden. "Our clients often asked for natural scents for their houses," says Urs Leuenberger, an interior architect who founded the label with colleague Romana Durisch. Alongside its premium scents, Arquinesia produces soaps, candles and shower gels.
arquinesia.com

SPECIALIST SHOP
KINIRIA
Menorca

Spain has a rich manufacturing heritage, especially when it comes to leather – and this tradition extends to Menorca (the island's singular sandals are sold worldwide). In Ciutadella, there's a designer working hard to keep the nation's craftsmanship alive: Eva Amat is a self-taught leatherworker and former environmental scientist who launched handbag brand Kiniria in 2008. Inside the shop, the smell of leather fills the air: this is where many of the bags are handmade, and rolls of soft material and tools are on show. "We create simple, functional designs with a Mediterranean essence," Amat says. "They are timeless."
kiniria.com

DESIGN & RETAIL

SPECIALIST SHOP
ORANGERIE
Seville

Evidence of Seville's blossoming creative scene can be found all over the city but the area around Alameda de Hércules is a particular hotbed for independent retail and hospitality. It's here that you'll find plant shop and florist Orangerie, founded by Juanma González in 2021. "I was surprised to discover that the province of Cádiz is close behind the Netherlands when it comes to flower exporting," says González. "Seventy per cent of our flowers come from the fields of the region." In the spirit of keeping things local, Orangerie supplies blooms for various businesses in the city.
+34 663 328 429

SPECIALIST SHOP
JAVIER S MEDINA CARPINTERIA 28
Madrid

Ostensibly, Javier S Medina makes decorative objects. In reality, he moulds esparto grass and wicker into crafts encompassing the worlds of fashion, design and art. "When you are creative, you can work in any sector," he says of his collaborations with brands including Zara and Loewe (*see page 107*). In 2013, he opened his store-cum-atelier where he weaves his best-known works – whimsical animal busts. Medina also hosts workshops, citing the importance of fostering community among artisans. "Beyond a particular piece, what we are all looking for is to understand the human behind it."
javiersmedina.com

DESIGN & RETAIL

SPECIALIST SHOP
CASA DE DIEGO
Madrid

When Fernando de Torre arrived in Madrid in 1823 from rainy Asturias he decided to sell what he knew best: umbrellas. But after his nephew Manuel took over, the brand expanded its range to include fans as an answer to Madrid's sweltering summer season. And that's what Casa de Diego is known for today. "Each fan is made in Valencia from the wood of fruit trees and handpainted," says sixth-generation owner Javier Llerandi de Inchaurza (*pictured, on right*). The shop is unassuming and adorned from floor to ceiling with fans, as well as shawls, canes and, of course, umbrellas.
casadediego.info

True fan
The folding fan that we know today originated in China, and was brought to Europe by Portuguese traders. It was later popularised in European courts and eventually became an essential element of flamenco dances.

SPAIN

SPECIALIST SHOP
COCOL
Madrid

When Pepa Entrena noticed that Spanish crafts were disappearing from Madrid's shops in place of mass-produced products from further afield, she was inspired to found Cocol, which opened its doors in 2016. Inside wooden shelves and tables are lined with objects large and small, but it's not your usual bric-a-brac – everything is handmade in Spain using traditional processes. Entrena sources products from every corner of the country: "I always meet the person behind it. It's important to me to have these personal relationships, because these products are personal."
cocolmadrid.es

DESIGN & RETAIL

SPECIALIST SHOP
CANDELA EN RAMA
Valencia

El Pilar in Valencia was once known for its abundance of silk workshops and looms. The weavers have long gone but the neighbourhood is once again popular with the city's artisans. One such creative is Candela Blasco, who opened her shop-cum-atelier in 2020 where she sells and crafts her elegant, Mediterranean-inspired jewellery. In fact, every piece is handmade in an adjoining atelier, where windows onto the street and shop provide customers with a view of Blasco at work. "Throughout history, jewellers' workshops have remained closed to the public. I always wanted passers-by to participate in what I'm creating," she says.
candelaenrama.com

SPECIALIST SHOP
CASA PONSOL
San Sebastián

On a busy corner in San Sebastián's old town is a hat shop founded by milliner Bernardo Ponsol in 1838, making it the town's oldest standing business – and the best-known spot to find the Basque iteration of a beret, *txapela*. Over the decades the store has experienced its share of ups and downs: it briefly supplied berets to King Alfonso XIII in the late 19th century and was forced to make military caps for the Falange during the civil war. Today the shop is run by sixth-generation owner Iñaki Leclercq Garcia and his mother Maria Pilar Garcia, both of whom can be found behind the original mahogany counter ready to help.
casaponsol.com

SPAIN

CONCEPT STORE
PERSUADE
Bilbao

"Making a multibrand shop work is much like putting together a flower arrangement," says owner Rosa Orrantia. "With so many different styles, colours and shapes at your disposal, you can create the perfect look for anyone." Orrantia's range of clothing, fragrances and antique items has drawn the upper echelons of Bilbao society since 1984 – and has become a design beacon in its own right. Persuade sells products by the likes of Sybilla, Jesús del Pozo, Yohji Yamamoto, Dries Van Noten and Martin Margiela. "We stock labels that share our commitment to utmost quality."
persuade.es

DESIGN & RETAIL

CONCEPT STORE
LLOP MADRID
Madrid

Álex Llop opened his shop-cum-gallery in 2021 following a 20-year career in the fashion industry, which took him from Japan to London. Stark white walls provide a perfect backdrop to a colourful array of sculptural candles, ceramics and artworks by emerging creatives. But the star of the show is Llop's clothing line: rails are dotted with elegant handmade pieces, from relaxed blazers to sumptuous knitwear. The clothing combines Llop's Spanish heritage with a minimal Japanese aesthetic.
llopmadrid.com

That's a wrap
Llop's aesthetic and sustainable ethos is based on Japanese consumerist culture, such as the concept of *furoshiki*: the traditional way of transporting goods by wrapping them in cloth.

SPAIN

MULTIBRAND FASHION
PEZ
Madrid

Though the Salesas district is now one of the capital's chicest hubs, it was off the beaten path when Patricia de Salas and Beatriz Mezquíriz (*both pictured, De Salas on right*) opened their multibrand shop there in 2004. Pez is now a cult favourite. They created a space that features labels including Ulla Johnson and Mirror in the Sky. De Salas explains how their tastes have developed: "Over time you begin to filter things out, and your eye becomes more discriminating. Your better-defined personality seeks out objects that fit more with who you are."
pez-pez.es

No place like home
Pez has a second location on the same street, stocking homeware. Here you'll find hand-woven linens, modern light fixtures and elegant ceramics by local brand Laon Pottery.

MULTIBRAND FASHION
SPORTIVO
Madrid

Since opening at the start of the 2000s, Madrid's Sportivo menswear shop has been operating on the principle that more is more. "Of course, it would make our lives easier to stock fewer brands," says manager Gustavo Perez Ruiz. "But minimalism has never been our thing." Sportivo sells more than 60 global brands from its two-storey shop on the corner of a pretty square in the city's Conde Duque neighbourhood. There's a mix of established and emerging brands on offer and the main focus is to bring the best of international design to Madrid. "We're always looking for new creative to add," says buyer Nacho López.
sportivostore.com

MULTIBRAND FASHION
BASSAL
Barcelona

Pol Bassal (*pictured*) decided to open his shop in Barcelona after noticing a lack of quality multi-label retailers in his hometown. "On a visit to Kyoto, I kept noticing all these really well-designed stores selling Japanese brands," he says. "I thought – that's exactly what my city is missing." In 2020 Bassal opened its doors, selling mostly womenswear from Spanish brands including Catalan shoemakers About Arianne and knitwear from Galicia-based Cordera. There is also a handful of international labels, such as shirts from Denmark's Jan Machenhauer. "Our range of brands is unique in the city," says Bassal. "Most of them can't be found anywhere else."
bassal.store

FASHION
LOREAK MENDIAN
San Sebastián

Meaning "flowers in the mountains", Loreak Mendian is inspired by the sea, surf and Basque culture. The clothing brand was co-founded by Victor Serna and Xabi Zirikiain in a northern fishing harbour in 1995. It has since grown into a practical and versatile label that has reached shoppers in London and Paris. It was important to Serna and Zirikiain – both surfers – to incorporate their laidback lifestyle into Loreak Mendian. Today, the pair's breezy approach can be felt in not only the collection but also in the bright minimalist shop, which is located two blocks from San Sebastián's iconic La Concha beach (*see page 165*).
loreakmendian.com

FASHION
MASSCOB
A Coruña, Galicia

A Coruña natives Jacobo Cobián and Marga Massanet were simply looking for a creative outlet when they founded women's ready-to-wear label Masscob in 2003. The brand's lines include loose dresses and blouses, boyish tailored trousers and easygoing jackets to wrap over your shoulders on the breezy summer nights typical of northern Spain. Everything is rendered in natural fabrics, including wool, linen, silk and cotton, by the brand's team of pattern-makers, fabric cutters and seamstresses and is designed to withstand the test of time. Masscob also work with artisans to produce limited handmade editions.
masscob.com

DESIGN & RETAIL

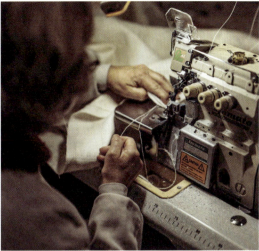

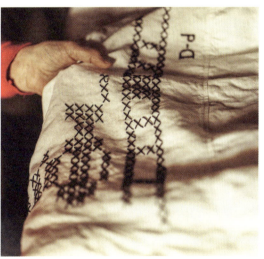

FASHION
D-DUE
Rianxo, Galicia

Having studied fashion in Barcelona and worked for years in Milan, Charo Froján returned to Galicia in 1994 to take over the skirt-making company that her parents had founded in the 1960s. Alongside her creative partner Alfredo Olmedo (*both pictured*), who joined the business in 2001, Froján channels Galicia's wildness in a range of pieces that are loose and primarily made of linen. Where Froján specialises in pattern-cutting, Olmedo pays more attention to the clothes' graphic elements, hand-painting some of D-due's unique pieces. "We see white linen as a blank canvas," he says.
d-due.com

Keeping things local
One of D-due's founding principles was to preserve Galicia's manufacturing traditions. The company's factory is just across the corridor from the design studio – as well as being useful for quick prototyping, having the production department so close ensures that jobs remain in the community.

FASHION
MAN 1924
Bilbao

Man 1924 is known among Spain's best-dressed for perfectly balanced traditional and contemporary clothing. Owner Jorge Navares, and his cousins Olga and Carlos Castillo, have overseen Man 1924's transformation from a small business opened by their grandfather in – you guessed it – 1924, to a global hit. The brand uses cotton from Italy and wool from Scotland, and the collections are made in Spanish and Portuguese factories. The entire range – from wedding suits to pyjamas – is designed in Bilbao. "We know everybody around here," says Jorge. "It's like they're part of the family."
man1924.com

In vogue
The Basque Country has produced its fair share of fashion big hitters – the likes of Paco Rabanne, Mercedes de Miguel and Cristóbal Balenciaga were all born in the region – the latter has a museum dedicated to his legacy on the coast near San Sebastián.

DESIGN & RETAIL

FASHION
LOEWE
Madrid

In 1846, a cooperative of craftspeople came together to make beautiful handmade leather objects. Today, as part of the LVMH Group, Loewe has updated its designs to include clothing for men and women while staying true to its traditions: luxury accessories continue to be handmade in Spain. The interiors of Casa Loewe, the brand's flagship store on Calle Serrano in Madrid, have been designed to resemble an art collector's apartment. Under the creative direction of designer Jonathan Anderson, the brand has settled into a space where art and fashion can inform one another. "It is interesting for Loewe to show what is possible within applied craft," says Anderson.
loewe.com

FASHION
CAPAS SESEÑA
Madrid

Full-length capes were all the rage in Madrid in the 19th century. In 1901, when the outerwear had neared the end of its sartorial dominance, Capas Seseña opened with the vision that a true classic never goes out of style. Marcos Seseña represents the fourth generation of a family that has kept the made-to-order, merino-wool capes alive for more than 120 years. Newer models feature shorter lengths, updated fabrics and details such as pockets for a more "casual" look, Seseña says. "Many clients come in thinking they'll love the modern capes but end up buying our classics – thus, somehow, the classic cape remains our top seller."
sesena.com

FASHION
OTEYZA
Madrid

Paul García de Oteyza and Caterina Pañera consider themselves outsiders in the world of bespoke tailoring. Though neither studied fashion before opening the shop in 2011, the impeccable fit and daring cuts of their garments prove that they are quick studies. "A true tailor needs 10 years in a workshop to learn the trade," says Pañera, a former translator whose grandfather and great-grandfather both worked in the industry. While the brand's foundations are in made-to-measure suits that reveal an enthusiasm for Spain's traditional silhouettes, Oteyza now has a prêt-à-porter line (almost exclusively made in Spain) created for an international clientele who might not have the time to visit the Madrid workshop for a full fitting. *deoteyza.com*

DESIGN & RETAIL

FASHION
ECOALF
Madrid

Words such as "waste" and "plastic" usually bring to mind landfill sites, a perception that Javier Goyeneche has been trying to change through his sustainable fashion brand Ecoalf since 2009. "Our mission has been to create a new generation of recycled products with the same quality and design as the best non-recycled," he says. Since its launch, Ecoalf has transformed 275 million plastic bottles into a sustainable collection that counts T-shirts and knitwear to yoga mats and suitcases. In 2022 the brand also debuted a new luxury clothing range, Ecoalf 1.0.
ecoalf.com

SHOES
ALONSO
Bilbao

On the corner of Calles Colón de Larreátegui in Bilbao's city centre, men's shoe shop Alonso stands out as one of the vestiges of the city's well-dressed bygone era. Despite the changing times, the shop hasn't lost any of its old charm: "We haven't changed anything from the initial design. The furniture, the light fixtures, the chairs – they are all original," says owner Cristina Alonso Jiménez, whose grandfather opened the shop in 1940. A longstanding relationship with local brands and manufacturers allows Alonso to make changes to footwear, from the leathers to soles, meaning many of the shoes on offer are one of a kind.
calzadosalonso.com

SHOES
HEREU
Barcelona

Hereu was founded in 2014 by José Bartolomé and Albert Escribano. The Barcelona-based brand is known for its chunky loafers and woven-leather handbags. "Our first styles were reinterpretations of traditional footwear from the Balearic Islands and everything evolved from there," says Bartolomé. "When it comes to new designs, we search for factories with a particular craft or technique that they've been doing for a long time, and then create something from that."
hereustudio.com

SHOES
CASTAÑER
Banyoles, Cataluña

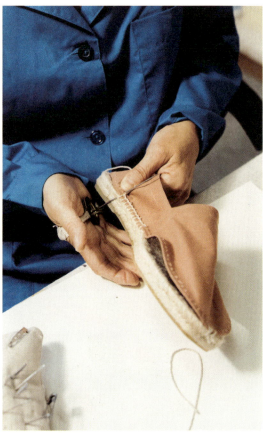

The humble espadrille – whose name derives from *esparto*, the tough grass traditionally braided to make its sole – was originally worn by peasants in farming communities in the Pyrenees. Luís Castañer and his cousin Tomàs Serra founded their espadrille workshop in 1927 (and the company was nationalised during the Spanish Civil War in order to provide footwear for the Republican soldiers) but the post-war industrialisation that swept across Spain meant the style more or less fell out of use. The brand's fortunes changed in the 1970s when it was approached by Yves Saint Laurent, who wanted to produce a wedged version of the shoe – thus elevating the espadrille from a practical piece of footwear to the fashion statement it is today.
castaner.com

DESIGN & RETAIL

SHOES
PEDRO GARCÍA
Madrid

SHOES
GLENT
Madrid

Glent, founded in 2014, specialises in custom-made men's shoes by combining Spanish craftsmanship with cutting-edge technology. Customers' feet are measured instore using a 3D laser scanner that calculates their precise shape and size. "A lot of knee and hip problems are caused by bad footwear," says company director Carlos Baranda. Glent employs a team of podiatrists who make sure that the product meets a customer's specific needs. The loafers can also be personalised: there are 60 models to choose from, as well as various options for leather, lining and sole. Every pair is handmade in Spain and the brand also offers a maintenance service too.
glentshoes.com

Pedro García started his eponymous footwear label in 1925 with the opening of a children's shoe workshop in Elda, Alicante – in the heart of Spain's shoe-making industry. The company grew into an international brand through its uncompromising quality and distinctive embellishments. Today, it is run by the third generation, siblings Pedro and Mila, and sells its footwear in more than 1,000 shops worldwide – including its Madrid flagship. The designs, which range from heeled sandals to clogs, focus as much on elegance as their ease of wear. All pairs are made by skilful *zapateros* in the Alicante factory.
pedrogarcia.com

Spain has a long history of designing and making but there's a new generation of creatives shaking up the industry. Here we meet three of them.

MEET THE EXPERTS

ARTIST & DESIGNER
JAIME HAYON
Hayon Studio

Jaime Hayon launched his creative studio in 2000 and has worked with Cartier, Cassina and Fritz Hansen.

Tell us about the design scene in Spain.
Spain has a beautiful design scene, especially in Valencia and Barcelona where there seems to be a different approach. But the scene has changed over the past decade. More restaurants, cafés and galleries are considering interior design and placing importance on it. When I was growing up, design didn't seem very relevant. Today, it plays a huge role. It is even being implemented by the Spanish government – from city logos to the introduction of Madrid's Design Festival.

What influences your work?
Conversations, history, craftmanship and colour. I love to pick up new techniques when I'm travelling and adding my own modern twist.

Where do you go in Spain for good art, culture and design?
There is so much on offer in the main cities Madrid, Barcelona and Valencia, which is where I live. But you shouldn't forget about Málaga, Seville, San Sebastián and Bilbao. There's so much variety in Spain. Every time I visit the Balearic Islands, they seem to be more cultural. Ibiza, Menorca and Mallorca are producing incredible art, with lots of interesting initiatives.

DESIGN & RETAIL

RETAILERS
JAVIER & MARIA ROSA GONZÁLEZ
Casa González & González

Shop owners Javier and Maria Rosa González collect objects that are made without haste and designed to last.

How did Casa Gonzalez & Gonzalez begin?
We met when we were children in Extremadura and would play together in the countryside. Javier became an interior designer and I [Maria Rosa] worked in museums and galleries. Many years later we were living in Madrid and noticed a gap the market in Spain for simple, timeless items. We decided to start the business selling a curated selection of goods from around the world.

What has inspired your business?
We're influenced by the Japanese Mingei movement and the Shakers' aesthetic in America. Our upbringing in Extremadura has had an impact on our project with a slower and more sensitive approach to materials and well-made goods; our tiny shop is a mix of that.

Tell us about your products.
We have a selection of functional, genuine objects for daily use such as homeware and personal care products. We believe our objects can transform a daily task into something enjoyable. We also have our own line of products such as ceramics and candle holders.

MANUFACTURER
OSCAR NAVARRO CRIADO
Crunat

Oscar Navarro Criado is the owner of Alicante-based shoe and handbag manufacturing company Crunat.

How did Crunat begin?
I was working as an architect but decided to move on to new challenges. My partner Florencia de la Cruz is a shoe designer and together we decided to create a shoe brand. We started with a thorough search for manufacturers. At first we looked at India but soon we realised that the best craftsmanship was to be found in Spain. We decided to set up and focus on our own production line beginning with footwear production and then handbags.

Why did you choose to set up shop in Elche?
It is the heart of the Spanish shoemaking industry so there is a vast pool of suppliers and talent here.

What brands do you work with?
We are currently working with Canadian brands, such as Maguire as well as Spanish labels including Bimani. Our customers may come from different countries, but they all share the same demand: the highest standards for design and finish.

What have you learned since opening Crunat?
Finding reliable professionals is key. Also, having a deep insight of the business is necessary before venturing into manufacturing for others. Ideally, you should start with your own brand, and then, work for others once you have learned from all the failures at your own expense.

SPAIN

We've compiled a round-up of our favourite Spanish products to help you pick out the perfect souvenir – from handmade ceramics and a pair of leather sandals to a Santa & Cole classic.

THE SHOPPING LIST

1. ColaCao chocolate drink
   colacao.es
2. Emilio Arias Lizano sunflower seeds
   emilioariaslizano.com
3. Ceramic jug from Canoa Lab
   canoalab.com
4. Ortiz canned tuna
   conservasortiz.com
5. Nuñez de Prado olive oil
   aceitesdobaena.com
6. Palmaria soap
   palmaria-mallorca.com

114

DESIGN & RETAIL

1 Sargadelos candelabra
  sargadelos.com
2 Earthenware water jug from Cocol
  cocolmadrid.es
3 Sargadelos coffee set
  sargadelos.com
4 Pallarès Solsona knives
  pallaressolsona.com
5 Fan from Casa de Diego
  casadediego.info

1. Bicoca table lamp from Marset
   marset.com
2. Lacuesta vermouth
   martinezlacuesta.com
3. Bowl from Cerámica los Arrayanes
   ceramicalosarrayanes.com
4. Estrella Galicia beer
   estrellagalicia.es
5. Mahou beer
   mahou.com
6. Cafés Pozo coffee
   cafedromedario.com
7. Al Júcar saffron
   azafranesmanchegos.com
8. La Purísima paprika
   la-purisima.es
9. Rafael Andreu chocolate
   chocolatesrafaelandreu.com

DESIGN & RETAIL

1. Pesca sandals from Hereu
   hereustudio.com
2. Flamenco Pocket in nappa calfskin from Loewe
   loewe.com
3. Ábbatte blanket
   abbatte.com
4. Cestita lamp from Santa & Cole
   santacole.com
5. Leather belt from Cocol
   cocolmadrid.es
6. Traditional taracea box from Artesanía González
   granadataracea.com

1 Brush from Cocol
cocolmadrid.es
2 Pablo espadrilles from Castañer
castaner.com
3 Basket bag in palm leaf and calfskin from Loewe
loewe.com
4 Horno Santo Cristo ensaimada
hornosantocristo.com
5 Xocolata Jolonch hot chocolate
xocolatajolonch.com
6 Handpainted tile from Tenderete Sevilla
tenderete-sevilla.negocio.site
7 Vintage painted house number from Populart
populartsevilla.com

DESIGN & RETAIL

1 Bodegas Habla 19 red wine
   bodegashabla.com
2 Arroz Catalá Valencia paella rice
   +34 961 751 144
3 Garcima enamelled paella pan
   garcima.com
4 El Obrador de Antequera
   piquitos artesanos
   piquitosartesanos.com
5 Sidonia rustic breadsticks
   picossidonia.com
6 Casa Mira turrón
   casamira.es
7 Casa Mariol black vermouth
   casamariol.com

SPAIN

1. Bàrbara Forés Abrisa't white wine
   cellerbarbarafores.com
2. El Maestro Sierra sherry
   maestrosierra.com
3. Perelló pitted olives with chilli
   perellofoods.com
4. Xoriguer Mahon Gin
   xoriguer.es
5. Flor de Calasparra rice
   arrozdecalasparra.es
6. Ceramic bowl from Cocol
   cocolmadrid.es
7. Almond slices from
   El Súper de los Pastores
   elsuperdelospastores.com

DESIGN & RETAIL

THE SHOPPING LIST

DISCOVER SPAIN

1. Lukan Gourmet squid stuffed peppers
   tienda.lukangourmet.com
2. Bernardo Estévez Chánselus red wine
   aterraagradececho.com
3. Balea sardines
   conservaslagopaganini.com
4. Capullo piquillo pepper marmalade
   conservascapullo.com
5. Gómez Cruzado Honorable Rioja
   gomezcruzado.com
6. La Picona salsa brava
   unionsalsera.com

With its fiestas, flamenco and first-class museums, Spain has plenty to offer culture fans. Here's our pick of the must-visit museums, galleries, music venues and more.

CULTURE

Under Francisco Franco's dictatorship, Spain promoted itself as the land of flamenco and bullfighting. The mystique created out of that Andalucian-tinged romanticism has persisted as a vision of Spain as a whole. Recently, however, musicians and artists have been promoting the rich diversity of other regional traditions. This is a long-standing practice in Spain, the blending of tradition with fresh perspectives, that stems from Catholic rituals – communities have developed festivities around religious events that add allegorical and satirical twists, imbuing those moments with their particular cultural perspectives. Over the centuries, Spain has been home to co-existing landscapes and languages that have allowed room for one another while also inspiring each other. It will come as no surprise then, that the country which gave the world Picasso, Dalí and Miró boasts an enviable collection of museums, galleries and cultural centres. Let's get better acquainted.

THE EDIT

1 **Museums**
The venues to visit, from the spaces dedicated to Spanish masters to striking structures in unexpected places.

2 **Cultural centres**
Three sites offering an avant-garde approach to the arts, including rooftop concerts, theatrical performances, workshops and more.

3 **Galleries**
Discover new creative talent at four commercial exhibition spaces.

4 **Music**
Explore the sounds of Spain, from authentic flamenco to the classic notes of the Tenerife Symphony Orchestra.

5 **Bookshops**
The independent and eclectic stores dedicated to print.

6 **The experts**
Dip into Spain's cultural world with notes from an editor, a gallerist and a musician.

CULTURE

MUSEUM
CASA MUSEO SALVADOR DALÍ
Portlligat, Cataluña

In 1930, Salvador Dalí bought a small beachside hut in the fishing village of Portlligat near Cadaqués. He lived in this remote corner of northeastern Cataluña until the early 1980s and, over the years, expanded the house into a sprawling, labyrinthine home linked by narrow corridors. In 1997, almost a decade after his death, the house became a museum run by the Dalí Foundation, which preserved all its original interiors. The space is something of a cabinet of curiosities, with gilded candelabras, taxidermied birds and porcelain vases arranged haphazardly throughout its white-washed walls.
salvador-dali.org

MUSEUM
CHILLIDA LEKU
Hernani, Basque Country

This sculpture park is dedicated to Basque artist Eduardo Chillida. Visitors can wander among more than 40 of his most inspired pieces and the 16th-century farmhouse once owned by the artist and his wife. The property was purchased by the couple in 1980 and they spent the next 15 years delicately restoring it and turning the scenic grounds into an open-air exhibition space (which opened to the public in 2011). "This is a reflection of Basque culture, the landscape and of Chillida's dedicated spirit of giving back," says museum director Mireia Massagué.
museochillidaleku.com

On the rocks
At the western end of San Sebastián's La Concha beach you'll find Chillida's "Haizearen Orrazia" (Comb of the Wind) – an installation of three 11-tonne steel sculptures which jut out of the rocks, dashed by the waves.

CULTURE

MUSEUM
FUNDACIÓ JOAN MIRÓ
Barcelona

Good together
Espai 13 – a smaller space within the gallery – exhibits works by contemporary artists that complement Miró's oeuvre, as well as guest works by the likes of Alexander Calder.

Perched high on the Montjuïc hillside overlooking Barcelona sits this museum and gallery dedicated to Catalan artist Joan Miró. It opened in 1975 in a structure purpose-built by architect Josep Lluís Sert, one of Miró's close friends who cut his teeth working with Le Corbusier. His idiosyncratic, asymmetric design is considered a landmark of rationalist architecture. Inside is the largest collection of the artist's work with more than 200 paintings, 169 statues and some 8,000 drawings. The foundation also organises exhibitions by emerging artists.
fmirobcn.org

SPAIN

MUSEUM
MACA
Alicante

In the shadow of Alicante's ninth-century Santa Bárbara castle sits the Museo de Arte Contemporáneo de Alicante (Maca), which opened in 2011. The museum took the place of La Asegurada, which was inaugurated in 1976 by Spanish sculptor Eusebio Sempere and was one of the first and most important modern art galleries in Spain. Maca is housed in the same building, a former 17th-century palace, which now includes a striking modern wing as well as a glass ceiling and atrium. The result is a light-filled interior providing the perfect home to some 800 20th-century pieces.
maca-alicante.es

MUSEUM
GUGGENHEIM MUSEUM BILBAO
Bilbao

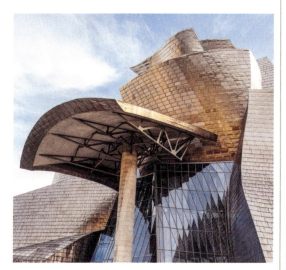

The story of modern Bilbao is perhaps the most accurate representation of the phrase: "If you build it, they will come." Following a period of steady decline in the city this iconic museum designed by Canadian-American architect Frank Gehry opened in 1997. The titanium and glass structure acted as a catalyst for art and culture in the city by integrating creativity into everyday life and today the institution receives some 3,000 visitors every day. Bilbao itself has transformed into a cosmopolitan destination with a buoyant economy – a phenomenon that has become known internationally as the "Bilbao effect".
guggenheim-bilbao.eus

MUSEUM
MUSEU PICASSO
Barcelona

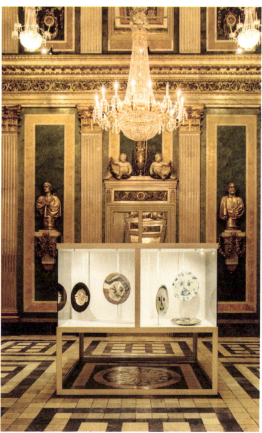

Pablo Picasso may have been born in Málaga but he spent much of his early life in Barcelona. His family moved to the Catalan capital in 1895 when he was 14 years old, and he stayed in the city until his mid-twenties before leaving for Paris. Picasso kept strong ties to Barcelona and in 1963 he helped his friend and personal secretary Jaume Sabartés open this gallery in a medieval palace in the city's Born neighbourhood. Over the years it has expanded across the four adjoining palaces and has a vast permanent collection of some 4,000 works by the artist, predominantly from the early years of his career.
museupicasso.bcn.cat

MUSEUM
HAUSER & WIRTH MENORCA
Menorca

From the art behemoth responsible for exhibition spaces from New York to Monaco comes Hauser & Wirth Menorca. Set on a islet in Mahón's harbour, this gallery and its tranquil gardens opened in 2021. Visitors must take a short ferry ride to reach Illa del Rei, where a restored 18th-century naval hospital has been reimagined by Argentine architect Luis Laplace. As well as the cavernous exhibition space, this artful outpost boasts a sculpture trail (with works by Eduardo Chillida and Joan Miró), as well as Cantina, a restaurant run by local winery Binifadet.
menorca.hauserwirth.com

CULTURE

Wine and dine
Binifadet, the winery that runs the onsite bistro, has its own restaurant at its vineyard in Sant Lluís. Visit for a long lunch with enough time to sample the alcoholic offerings.

MUSEUM
FUNDACIÓN NMAC
Vejer de la Frontera, Andalucía

MUSEUM
MUSEU CAN FRAMIS
Barcelona

The non-profit Fundació Vila Casas was founded in 1986 by pharmaceutical entrepreneur Antoni Vila Casas with the aim to champion contemporary Catalan art; today it operates five gallery spaces across the region. One of these venues is Museu can Framis, which opened in 2009 in a complex of 18th-century industrial buildings restored by architecture studio Baas, whose design comprises factory buildings and concrete exhibition halls. The collection spans some 300 works by Catalan artists dating from the 1960s onwards, with pieces from Joan Ponç and Antoni Tàpies among others.
fundaciovilacasas.com

The pine forest that is home to the NMAC unfolds across 30 hectares. The open-air contemporary art museum, opened in 2001, facilitates a dialogue between nature and art that allows visitors to appreciate how subtle changes in light and landscape impact their appreciation of installations. Works include those of James Turrell and Marina Abramovic, as well as local artists such as Jacobo Castellano: his sculpture "Viga Madre" is an homage to the migratory birds that return time and again as they fly between Europe and Africa.
fundacionnmac.org

CULTURE

MUSEUM
HELGA DE ALVEAR
Cáceres, Extremadura

German-born gallerist Helga de Alvear moved to Spain in the 1950s and has since gathered one of Europe's most important collections of contemporary art. In 2002 she donated all 3,000 works to the city of Cáceres on the condition that it build a museum. Part of the collection, which includes pieces by Picasso, Joseph Beuys and Olafur Eliasson, was previously shown at an old building but a new extension designed by Spanish architects Mansilla & Tuñón opened in 2021. Entrance is free and visitors are encouraged to get close to the art – there are no rope barriers in sight.
museohelgadealvear.com

MUSEUM
MUSEO REINA SOFÍA
Madrid

While home to a vast collection of 20th-century artwork, the Reina Sofía's primary draw remains "Guernica", Pablo Picasso's emotive painting. Visitors can also view pieces by other Spanish artists including Salvador Dalí, as well as those from further afield such as Anish Kapoor and Wassily Kandinsky. The museum's structure is a juxtaposition of diverging periods of architecture: a former 18th-century hospital in a neoclassical style is home to the main galleries while the adjoining 21st-century black and red edifice by architect Jean Nouvel has the futuristic feel of a space station.
museoreinasofia.es

MUSEUM
CAAC
Seville

Many visitors to Seville never venture across the bottle-green Río Guadalquivir but it's worth making a trip to the river's west bank for this charming contemporary art gallery alone. The Centro Andaluz de Arte Contemporáneo was founded in 1990 and boasts a permanent collection with works from the likes of Louise Bourgeois and Rebecca Horn scattered throughout the 15th-century former monastery. Don't miss the enigmatic "Alicia", a site-specific piece by Spanish artist Cristina Lucas, which features a giant figure protruding from the windows of the building.
caac.es

CULTURE

SPAIN

CULTURAL CENTRE
LA CASA ENCENDIDA
Madrid

In this cultural centre, visitors are not relegated to the distant observation of art. What began in 2002 as a space to support young artists today serves as a vibrant stage for interaction between avant-garde art and the community. The *neomudéjar* building (a revival of the Iberian Islamic style), constructed in 1913, revolves around an interior courtyard often used as an exhibition and performance space. La Casa Encendida hosts workshops related to environmental and sociological issues, and features a varied cultural agenda for audiences of all ages, including concerts on its rooftop terrace.
lacasaencendida.es

All in a name
La Casa Encendida (meaning The Illuminated House) is taken from a book of the same name by Spanish poet Luis Rosales Camacho.

CULTURAL CENTRE
CENTRO BOTÍN
Santander

In the 1960s, insurance magnate Marcelino Botín Sanz de Sautuola and his wife Carmen Yllera decided to start the Fundación Botín to build social and cultural wealth in Cantabria. Five decades later, the arts centre Centro Botín opened its doors, instantly becoming a local icon in its central location beside Santander Bay. Designed by Pritzker Prize-winning architect Renzo Piano and completed in 2017, the structure is elevated as if primed for takeoff and divided into two sections. The western wing has two exhibition rooms dedicated to art while the second section is used for cultural and educational activities with auditorium seating for up to 300 people.
centrobotin.org

CULTURAL CENTRE
UNIVERSIDAD LABORAL DE GIJÓN
Gijón, Asturias

Originally designed as an orphanage for children whose parents died in mining accidents, the Universidad Laboral de Gijón dates back to 1946, when architect Luis Moya Blanco designed a building that would symbolise recovery from the dark days of the civil war. The result was one of the biggest stone constructions ever made in Spain, housing a church, an institute of education, a broadcasting company and the tallest stone tower in the country. After a renovation, the building reopened in 2007 as a cultural centre with a café and restaurant. Visitors can climb the tower for sweeping views of the botanical gardens, mountains and coast.
laboralciudaddelacultura.com

ART GALLERY
DELIMBO
Seville

Seville's Delimbo gallery proves that there is much more to the cultural life of the southern city than flamenco and Velázquez. Founders Laura Calvarro and Seleka Muñoz have a background in graffiti and street art, and work with Spanish artists such as Matías Sánchez and Cristina Lama as well as international names including Momo, Alex Brewer and Vhils. Expect bold, colourful works displayed across the stark white space in a modernist building designed by José Espiau y Muñoz in 1919.
delimbo.com

ART GALLERY
PELAIRES
Mallorca

Opened by gallerist Pep Pinya in 1969, Pelaires is the longest-running contemporary art gallery in Spain. It debuted work by Joan Miró, Pablo Picasso and Antoni Tàpies, and was the first gallery in Spain to showcase work by foreign artists such as Alexander Calder. In the 1990s it relocated to an emblematic two-storey 17th-century building where it holds year-round exhibitions. Now run by second-generation owner Frederic Pinya (*pictured*), the gallery focuses on introducing the work of young international artists to Mallorca and wider Spain.
pelaires.com

ART GALLERY
ESPACIO VALVERDE
Madrid

ART GALLERY
ALZUETA
Barcelona

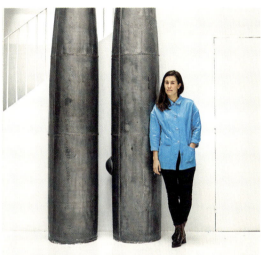

Asela Pérez Becerril founded Espacio Valverde in 2007, in a late 19th-century building (where horse-drawn carriages were once stored) complete with a labyrinthine collection of rooms and central courtyard reserved for artistic performances. "It has a certain spontaneity. We touch on all aspects of creativity," she says. The seeds for the gallery were planted when Pérez Becerril began hosting cultural events that ranged from theatrical shows to cultural talks. This led to her opening the fully-fledged gallery with her partner Jacobo Fitz-James Stuart. Today, it focuses on artworks that allow viewers to experience the world in a fresh way.
espaciovalverde.com

Alzueta has been a key player in the evolution of Barcelona's contemporary art scene since opening in 2001. Its founder, Miquel Alzueta, spent more than 20 years working as a publisher before launching the gallery in a former textile factory. Over the years the enterprise has expanded to include a second location in the city as well as an outpost in Madrid and a gallery space in a 16th-century farmhouse on the Costa Brava. "It's an evolving project that tries to combine modernity, beauty and thought," says Alzueta. "The gallery always looks for artists from different fields but who stand out for their excellence."
alzuetagallery.com

LIVE MUSIC
TABANCO EL PASAJE
Jerez de la Frontera, Andalucía

Dating back to the 17th century, the *tabanco* is a traditional Jerez bar where bulk-wine is sold and served from casks of locally-produced varieties. As flamenco is deeply entrenched in the city's culture due to its Roma population, it's common for patrons to break out into song and dance. *Tabancos* were dying out by 2010 when Antonio Ramírez set out to restore his hometown's oldest exemplar: Tabanco El Pasaje, founded in 1925. "Flamenco is sold abroad, yet people would come to Jerez and couldn't find it as a daily occurrence," he says. As a response he now ensures that El Pasaje has at least two to three live performances each day.
tabancoelpasaje.com

LIVE MUSIC
PALAU DE LA MÚSICA CATALANA
Barcelona

Barcelona's Palau de la Música Catalana is one of the most exuberant examples of *modernisme* (also known as Catalan art nouveau). The design of architect Lluís Domènech i Montaner, the concert hall was built in the 1900s with no expense spared and there's hardly a surface that isn't dripping in ornamentation. Intricate mosaics and fantastical carvings stretch across its red-brick exterior, and its auditorium is topped by a vast blue-and-yellow stained-glass skylight. Every minute detail of Domènech i Montaner's design has been perfectly preserved and the space remains a popular spot for classical and contemporary live music.
palaumusica.cat

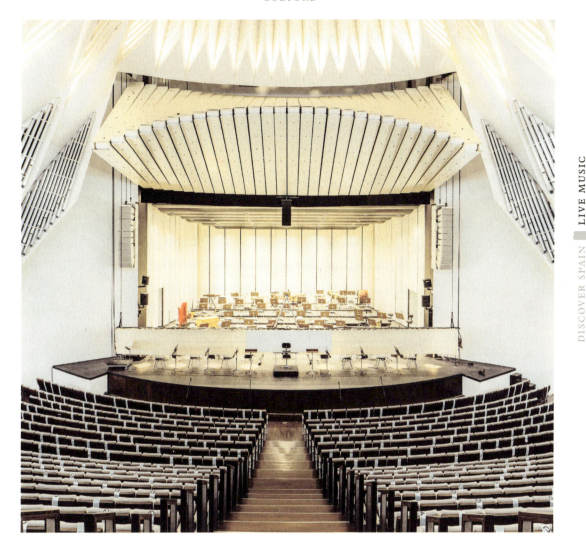

LIVE MUSIC
AUDITORIO DE TENERIFE
Tenerife

Arguably the most striking building on the island, the Auditorio de Tenerife was an attempt by Santiago Calatrava to create a structure that could rival the dramatic natural surroundings. Located near the port of Santa Cruz, the auditorium opened in 2003 to house the Tenerife Symphony Orchestra. Its imposing silhouette, often compared to a sail or a wave, has become a recognisable symbol of Tenerife and the building has established itself as the centre of the island's cultural scene, with regular dance, theatre and opera productions taking place in its 1800-seat hall.
auditoriodetenerife.com

SPAIN

BOOKSHOP
PAPERGROUND
Madrid

Magazine and bookshop Paperground might be housed in a pint-sized location, but its vibrant yellow frontage means that it's hard to miss. Inside, shoppers can choose from an array of international publications as well as a selection of books focusing on art and design. It's a world the two founders know well: Margherita Visentini is a freelance journalist and editor of *Polpettas on Paper* magazine, and Asier Rua (*both pictured*) is a photographer who also runs his own publishing business, Rua Ediciones. "Spain's independent publishing scene has really grown over the past few years," says Rua. "Paperground is a way of celebrating that."
Calle de Medellín 4

BOOKSHOP
LIBRERÍA TERRANOVA
Barcelona

Terranova began life in 2013 as a production company founded by filmmaker Luis Cerveró. "I knew a lot of photographers and artists in Barcelona who wanted to make books but there wasn't a publishing house that was willing to do it," says Cerveró. "So I decided to start my own." In 2020, Cerveró and business partner Lucía Boned set about transforming a historic shoe shop in the Sant Antoni neighbourhood into a space from which to sell their own publications alongside other art and photography books from around the world. There's also a small gallery space in the back that hosts regular exhibitions from local creatives.
terrranova.com

BOOKSHOP
LIBRERÍA DONOSTI
San Sebastián

This bookshop has occupied a corner of San Sebastián since Santiago and Conchita Azurmendi opened it in 1971. Today their children Santi and Andoni (and his wife Nuria) continue to run the business, although Conchita still frequents the shop and is always ready to chat to customers. "We are a family of great readers and we like to share our literary discoveries with our clients," says Santi. Librería Donosti stocks everything from children's books to literary fiction, with a small English section. The bookshop's main feature, however, is the green-painted exterior and art nouveau stained-glass window which stands out like a beacon across the plaza.
+34 943 424 688

While flamenco and Picasso might be some of Spain's best-known cultural exports, there's a further burgeoning creative scene to explore. We meet three plucky professionals shaking up the industry.

MEET THE EXPERTS

EDITOR & JOURNALIST
JAVIER MORENO BARBER
Print media

Javier Moreno Barber is the former editor in chief of Spain's most circulated daily newspaper, *El País*.

What role does 'El País' play in Spain?
When it launched, in 1976, *El País* had a very clear idea of what Spain should be (and was not, back then): an open, full democracy as well as a progressive, forward-looking society, where everyone could have a voice and everyone's rights would be respected.

What does the newspaper do differently to others?
Two things. It has a bigger newsroom of about 400 journalists which allows the newspaper to cover issues with the depth that readers demand nowadays. Plus it has a strong presence in Latin America, with a big newsroom in Mexico City and multiple bureaux with many journalists across the continent.

What is the future of print media?
Readers still love a print newspaper, especially weekend editions, and magazines. But readerships are moving online – and newspapers need to respond.

MUSICIAN
BIKÔKÔ
Soul and R&B

Barcelona-based musician Bikôkô has made her mark with a fusion of R&B and West African rhythms.

Tell us about the music scene in Spain.
Spain is a very interesting country and its music scene is so rich. The industry is not always the most diverse and open, so when I was growing up I didn't really relate to music here. But the more I travel, the more that I realise how vibrant Spanish culture is, and how many great musicians we have.

What are your influences?
I've always been in contact with music because my dad is a musician, and I grew up loving R&B and music by the likes of Erykah Badu and D'Angelo. My father is from Cameroon and I love West African music. In fact it has inspired my music a lot. Recently though I've expanded my influences to include musicians such as Rosalía, Fela Kuti and Björk, as well as West African music from the 1960s to the 1980s. I also love flamenco.

Any tips for finding live music in Barcelona?
It's a little hidden at first, but there's an up and coming music scene in the city. Go to the nearest bar and ask what's going on and you'll find lots of live music, from jazz bars to spontaneous events.

GALLERIST
NACHO RUIZ
Galería T20

Nacho Ruiz is the co-owner of T20 contemporary art gallery in the historic city of Murcia.

What was the inspiration behind launching a gallery?
I launched T20 with my partner Carolina Parra in 2000. We wanted to participate in the art of our time, create a platform for new creative trends and carve a cultural scene in Murcia that could link to the international art world.

What role do international art fairs play in your gallery?
Working from the small city of Murcia, art fairs are essential for us. We have participated in roughly 80 fairs since 2000, from Paris Photo and Zona Maco in Mexico to Volta and Artissima. This has given us an international position for our artists. The fairs, apart from benefitting the business, are also really fun with exciting weeks of meeting people, working and travelling.

Where do you go to view art in Spain?
Everywhere. There are monumental sites such as Toledo, Córdoba and Santiago de Compostela, but also small lost paradises including Genalguacil in Málaga and infinitely colourful landscapes, such as those of La Mancha. In Spain, you will find art in so many unexpected places.

What advice would you give to an aspiring gallerist in Spain?
A gallery is a business but it tends to be much more than that, it is a way of life. The risk is worth it, but bet on new looks and on current art.

Our round up of the ten buildings that truly showcase the innovation, creativity and sometimes pure eccentricity of Spain's built environment.

ARCHITECTURE

From Moorish masterpieces to modernist mansions, Spanish architecture tells the colourful story of the country itself. Muslim invasions, the rise of Christianity, the Renaissance and other outside influences have all left their mark on the nation's built environment. You'll find gothic cathedrals alongside Roman ruins and contemporary structures happily coexisting with baroque churches. Spanish architects have never been afraid to think outside the box: Gaudí's ornamental extravagance is probably the most famous example of this, with the colourful eccentricity of Ricardo Bofill's concrete constructions following firmly in his avant-garde footsteps. We've pulled together some of our favourite architectural feats and oddities to give you a flavour of the sheer range there is to see. Step inside to explore everything from a subterranean cultural complex in Lanzarote to artist Xavier Corberó's labyrinthine home in Barcelona.

THE EDIT

1 La Muralla Roja
Vibrant postmodern residential complex.

2 Casa Vicens
Gaudí's first residential commission is packed with natural motifs.

3 Ciudad de las Artes y las Ciencias
Calatrava's futuristic project changed Valencia's skyscape and fortunes.

4 Mezquita-Catedral de Córdoba
This breathtaking religious complex charts the history of Córdoba.

5 Torres Blancas
The 1960s housing complex that is still turning heads.

6 Espai Xavier Corberó
An Escher-esque structure which is now a house museum.

7 Jameos del Agua
One of Cesar Manrique's most enchanting projects on Lanzarote.

8 SGAE Central Office
This modern building made from slabs of granite looks almost prehistoric.

9 Museo Memoria de Andalucía
Granada's contemporary museum tells the story of the region.

10 Santuario de Arántzazu
A modernist basilica inspired by thorns.

RESIDENTIAL BUILDING
LA MURALLA ROJA
Calpe, Alicante

This apartment complex on the coast north of Benidorm was inspired by the geometric structures of North African kasbahs. Barcelona-born architect Ricardo Bofill – who completed over 1,000 projects at the helm of his firm RBTA – said he developed the concept over a period of 10 years prior to construction. The postmodern complex features vibrant red and pink exteriors, which contrast with the surrounding scrubland, while the interior spaces blend with the sea and sky in blues and purples. The interplay of blocky architectural elements, reminiscent of cubism, ensures that the building feels strikingly contemporary despite dating back to 1973.

MUSEUM
CASA VICENS
Barcelona

Adventurous, admirable and more than a little subversive, Antoni Gaudí is brand Barcelona's immortal poster child. This, his first residential commission, was conceived as a summer house for a wealthy stockbroker back in 1883. The building is permeated with natural motifs: floral forms adorn the ceilings, fruit is carved into the smoking room's Moorish-inspired concaves and painted majestic fauna grace the walls. Each room provides an insight into the ideas of a designer who would go on to shape the visual identity of an entire city. The house went under an extensive restoration project in 2017 and now functions as a museum.

ARCHITECTURE

CULTURAL COMPLEX
CIUDAD DE LAS ARTES Y LAS CIENCIAS
Valencia

Counting no less than six separate monolithic structures, Valencia's Ciudad de las Artes y las Ciencias (City of Arts and Sciences) is a feat of architectural design. Ultramodern and hard to miss, the sweeping site in the former Río Turia riverbed was the vision of architect Santiago Calatrava, who was awarded the project in 1991.

Completed in 2005 at a staggering cost of €1.2bn (blowing the initial estimate of €300m out of the water), the complex has more than lived up to its hefty price tag: the futuristic icon has attracted millions of visitors and played a significant role in the city's bid for World Design Capital in 2022.

RELIGIOUS SITE
MEZQUITA-CATEDRAL DE CÓRDOBA
Córdoba, Andalucía

Córdoba was once the capital of a vast Islamic state and one of the largest and most prosperous cities in the world. Abd al-Rahman I, founder of the Caliphate, built his original mosque in 785AD and over the centuries it evolved, blending different architectural styles. In 1236 Córdoba was captured by Christian forces and the mosque was converted into a cathedral, although only minor modifications were made until the 16th century when a Renaissance nave and transept were planted squarely in the centre. The defining feature of the complex remains a forest of more than 800 columns topped with terracotta and white striped double arches.

ARCHITECTURE

RESIDENTIAL BUILDING
TORRES BLANCAS
Madrid

Completed in 1969, Francisco Javier Sáenz de Oiza's high-density housing complex was leagues ahead of its time. Over 70 metres tall, the eccentric structure soared above the cheerless vernacular of Spain's entrenched dictatorship. Now, decades later, people are still marvelling at its audacity. The cylindrical trunk lined with curved balconies blossoms into a collection of full-blown discs on top, creating a platform for a rooftop garden and pool. Inspired in part by the work of Le Corbusier and Frank Lloyd Wright, the Spaniard went even further by applying his own style based on the natural growth patterns of trees.

MUSEUM
ESPAI XAVIER CORBERÓ
Barcelona

In 1967, Catalan artist Xavier Corberó bought an old farmhouse in his hometown of Esplugues de Llobregat on the fringes of Barcelona. He set about adding a vast, Escher-like extension to the house made up of some 300 concrete arches spanning out from an octagonal central courtyard. This complex provided studios and housing for artists-in-residence and was also used by Corberó as his atelier up until his death in 2017. Today the building is municipally owned and has been preserved as a house museum. It's also regularly used as a striking backdrop for photoshoots and performances: fashion brands from Miu Miu to Fendi have shot campaigns here.

ARCHITECTURE

CULTURAL COMPLEX
JAMEOS DEL AGUA
Lanzarote

Lanzarote-born César Manrique was a multidisciplinary architect, painter and sculptor who believed passionately that architecture should integrate respectfully with its natural environment. He campaigned tirelessly to make sure that Lanzarote resisted the high-rise development that had blighted so much of Spain's coast and his many projects across the island sit harmoniously within their surroundings. Jameos del Agua is no exception: the cultural complex – which includes a restaurant, bars, an auditorium and a swimming pool seemingly lifted from the lair of a James Bond villain – is built in and around a volcanic cave with a subterranean lake.

ARCHITECTURE

OFFICE BUILDING
SGAE CENTRAL OFFICE
Santiago de Compostela, Galicia

Running along one side of the Vista Alegre park in Santiago de Compostela is the Galician outpost of the General Society of Authors and Editors (SGAE). The organisation manages the copyrights of those working across Spain's cultural sphere and their space in the city is used to host a programme of activities, from readings and talks to plays and musical performances. The building, opened in 2007, is the design of Madrid-based Ensamble Studio who created a sculptural façade from uneven slabs of Mondariz granite. Behind this are the offices and function rooms, which descend two storeys below the visible structure.

MUSEUM
MUSEO MEMORIA DE ANDALUCÍA
Granada, Andalucía

After designing the Granada headquarters of Caja Granada bank in 2001, architect Alberto Campo Baeza was invited back several years later to add an adjoining museum of Andalucian history. The museum's exhibitions showcase the region's history and geography from Roman times to the present day.

Campo Baeza's design, which was inaugurated in 2009, includes a 10-storey tower with windows only at the eighth-floor restaurant and an internal courtyard with elliptical spiral ramps connecting the different levels. There's also a vast screen on one side of the tower where public showings of films and sporting events are held.

RELIGIOUS SITE
SANTUARIO DE ARÁNTZAZU
Oñati, Basque Country

According to local legend, the Virgin Mary once appeared amongst the hawthorns in this rugged area between Bilbao and San Sebastián, causing a shepherd to exclaim something along the lines of *"Arantzan zu!"* (Thou, among the thorns!). The shepherd subsequently insisted on building a sanctuary in her honour.

The structure itself has been twice destroyed by fire, and the latest reconstruction began in 1878. It wasn't until 1950 that the new basilica was added by modernist architects Francisco Javier Sáenz de Oiza and Luis Laorga. Their avant-garde design includes towers wrapped in stone studs inspired by thorns.

With some 3,000 beaches and 16 national parks spanning volcanic terrain to pristine sandy stretches, Spain has a bounty of natural spots to tempt you outside.

THE GREAT OUTDOORS

Few countries can boast such diverse landscapes as Spain. First there are the snow-tipped Pyrenees running along the French border and the dense greenery that spills out along the northern coast. The south is another world entirely: the sparse, rocky terrain of Almería was used as a stand-in for the Wild West in plenty of spaghetti westerns in the 1960s, and Cabo de Gata national park is Europe's only desert. Then there are the beaches: from the long swathes of sand along the Costa del Sol and the craggy, pine-lined coves of the Costa Brava to the windswept bays of Galicia, Spain is certainly not short of picturesque spots to plant your parasol. So grab your towel – or your hiking boots – it's time to explore.

THE EDIT

1 Natural parks
From pine-tree clad countryside to lunar-like terrain, Spain's open spaces are as varied as they are beautiful.

2 Beaches
Eight spectacular seaside spots including sandy urban stretches, wild islands and azure waters.

THE GREAT OUTDOORS

NATURAL PARK
TIMANFAYA
Lanzarote

The rugged landscape of Lanzarote's Timanfaya National Park was sculpted by a series of continuous volcanic eruptions in the 18th century. The result is its characteristic Mars-like terrain, which is almost completely devoid of vegetation and covers a quarter of the island's total land mass.

SPAIN

NATURAL PARK
PARQUE RURAL DE ANAGA
Tenerife

Emerging dramatically from the northeastern tip of Tenerife, this verdant mountain range is draped in subtropical vegetation. Parque Rural de Anaga offers explorers craggy peaks, deep ravines and laurel forests. The park has more than 100 hiking trails, some of which lead down to deserted black-sand beaches.

NATURAL PARK
PICOS DE EUROPA
Asturias, Cantabria and Castilla y León

The Picos de Europa mountain range sits at the edge of Asturias, Cantabria and Castilla y León. Dotted with oak and beech trees, the park is home to plenty of fauna (including native brown bears) and supposedly got its name from sailors as it was the first thing they would spot on their return to Europe from the Americas.

THE GREAT OUTDOORS

NATURAL PARK
PENÍNSULA DE LLEVANT
Mallorca

Mallorca's Península de Llevant is home to much of the Artà mountain range, as well as winding trails and hidden bays and beaches. The protected area is a wildlife haven that's inhabited by everything from booted eagles and peregrine falcons to tortoises, hedgehogs and pine martens.

BEACH
PLAYA LA CALETA
Cádiz, Andalucía

Cádiz sits at the end of a skinny peninsula and is almost entirely surrounded by water, so it's no surprise that the city's beaches play a large part in daily life. Locals head to La Caleta, a picturesque stretch of sand flanked by the San Sebastián and Santa Catalina castles to swim, socialise, eat or play a leisurely game of cards.

THE GREAT OUTDOORS

BEACH
ISLAS CÍES
Galicia

Galicia may not compete with the rest of Spain when it comes to hours of sunshine, but it is home to some of the country's most beautiful beaches. The Islas Cíes – a rocky archipelago off the coast of Vigo – have no cars, no hotels and strictly limited visitor numbers lending them an air of Robinson Crusoe remoteness.

BEACH
PLATJA DE SES ILLETES
Formentera

BEACH
PLATJA DE LA PATACONA
Valencia

Spain's third-largest city is perhaps its beachiest, with kilometres of sand easily accessible from the centre. Furthest from the busy palm-tree-lined promenade is Platja de la Patacona. Valencians head to this golden stretch for the lively *chiringuitos* (beach bars), volleyball courts and people-watching opportunities.

The crystal-blue waters and pinkish coral sand of Platja de Ses Illetes make it one of the most prized spots in Formentera. The postcard-perfect beach is located on a thin stretch of coastline to the island's north and is only a short hop on a boat from neighbouring Ibiza.

BEACH
PLAYA LA CONCHA
San Sebastián

San Sebastián may have made a name for itself as a food-lover's paradise but it has plenty to offer sun-worshippers too. Playa La Concha, a crescent-shaped stretch with views of Isla Santa Clara sits in the heart of the city and acts as a playground for sunbathers and surfers alike.

BEACH
PLAYA EL BOLLULLO
Tenerife

Though Tenerife is widely known for package holidays, its beaches aren't formed of the white sands and turquoise waters that people might expect: the shores of the volcanic island are almost exclusively inky-hued. On the northern coast, Playa el Bollullo is only accessible by foot but its wide, empty expanse is worth the hike.

BEACH
CALA MACARELLETA
Menorca

This secluded spot is another beach you'll have to don your trainers for: sun-seekers must trek Menorca's Camí de Cavalls, an ancient pine-tree-shaded path that encircles the entire island, from one of the nearby coves. The spoils more than make up for the hot slog: Cala Macarelleta offers some of the Med's most pristine waters.

BEACH
PLAYA DE LOS LANCES
Tarifa, Andalucía

Located at the southernmost tip of Spain, Tarifa is one of the world's premier destinations for wind sports – it is affectionately known among residents as The City of Wind. Playa de Los Lances is its nearest beach and offers both golden sands and crashing waves, blowing in kite surfers from around the world.

PART 02

PUT DOWN ROOTS

So you are considering staying a little longer – perhaps even settling down permanently? Allow us to introduce you to the best areas to invest in, the architects and designers to enlist plus a few people who have already made the move.

With its great transport links and sunny climate (and outlook),
Spain offers both ample business opportunities and great quality of life.
Here are some suggestions on where to set up shop.

WHERE TO LIVE

THE CREATIVE NEIGHBOURHOOD
RUZAFA
Valencia

Often overshadowed by Madrid and Barcelona, Spain's third largest city is relaxed, creative and full of joie de vivre. Ruzafa is one of its most desirable enclaves and has bags of potential.

Population: 840,000
Closest airport: Valencia Airport is a 20-minute drive
Eat: Canalla Bistro
Drink: Bluebell Coffee Roasters
Shop: Cuit Espai Ceràmic

Valencia enjoys one of the country's most agreeable climates, boasts vibrant cultural, gastronomic and design scenes and offers important transport links thanks to its train network and international airport. Furthermore, it handles 20 per cent of Spain's exports as one of Europe's busiest ports. But this coastal city also offers excellent quality of life: Valencians have access to 20km of pristine beaches, 150km of cycle paths and plentiful green spaces, not to mention its affordability (the cost of living here is 20 per cent lower than the country's capital).

One of Valencia's most desirable areas is Ruzafa, which has seen a boom since the 2010s with an influx of independent shops and restaurants. The area consistently proves popular with expats, in part thanks to an ambitious urban planning project (the first stage was completed in 2019) that will see the city's train lines move underground to make way for the new Parque Central. Old train sheds are also due to be converted into cultural spaces – one of which will house a gallery by modern art museum Ivam.

SPAIN

THE START-UP HUB
VIGO
Galicia

This northern port city is on the up, fast establishing itself as a home of entrepreneurship, technology and international trade – plus a blossoming tourism sector that still hasn't reached its full potential.

Population: 300,000
Closest airport: Santiago-Rosalía de Castro Airport is a 60-minute drive
Eat: La Carpintería
Drink: Cervexería Nós
Shop: Sargadelos

Sheltered by the Islas Cíes (*see page 163*), Galicia's largest city – home to nearly 300,000 inhabitants – has always been shaped by its strong connection to the water. Vigo's economy, however, is no longer solely reliant on the port's activities and the entire metropolitan region of Vigo has become a hub for new ideas and business ventures. This is in part thanks to the many conferences, international trade fairs and business-accelerator programmes that are being promoted by local government and institutions.

According to the region's chamber of commerce, more than 18,000 new companies were registered between 2020 and 2021.

Vigo makes the most of its strategic position on the edge of the Atlantic but head south and the border with neighbouring Portugal is only a 30-minute drive away and nearby Santiago de Compostela provides the crucial link with an international airport. Vigo has outgrown its old industrial label and today can proudly call itself a true business city.

THE COASTAL OUTPOST
TARIFA
Andalucía

Mainland Europe's southernmost tip is tempting a new crowd thanks to its quality of life, plentiful beaches and laidback ambience.

Population: 18,500
Closest airport: Gibraltar International Airport is a 50-minute drive
Eat: Bar El Frances
Drink: Número C
Shop: Zero Gravity

As continental Europe's southernmost city, Tarifa lies a mere 20km from Morocco and is further south even than the African capital cities of Algiers and Tunis across the water. In fact, it is possible to cross the strait by hydrofoil and arrive in Tangier in an hour. Tarifa's status as a far-flung port city continues to be a source of intrigue for many who are looking to escape the daily grind, live more simply and get closer to nature. Along the Playa de Los Lances (see page 167), many locals begin their day in motion; skaters and cyclists whizz past while kite surfers propel themselves across the edge of the sea. "It feels a bit like the Caribbean," says Eszter Felkai, the founder and head of a fashion PR agency. "It took me five years to find this place," she says. "In Tarifa, it is not so much a matter of finding a home with a certain amount of square metres; it is about the location, the light." The most desirable residential properties in and around Tarifa are either in the historic centre, overlooking the Playa de Los Lances, or in the countryside to the north and east of the city.

THE BUSINESS CITY
MÁLAGA
Andalucía

This southern city has more to offer than simply being the gateway to the Costa del Sol. In fact, Málaga is reinventing itself as a cultural and economic hub – and big global brands are moving in.

Population: 590,000
Closest airport: Málaga-Costa del Sol Airport is a 20-minute drive
Eat: La Cosmopolita Malagueña
Drink: Antigua Casa de Guardia
Shop: Mercado Central de Atarazanas

The sun rises above Málaga, melting away the mist that rolls off the Mediterranean. This is a typical start to the day on the Costa del Sol, named for its average 320 days per year of sunshine. Since this stretch of Andalucian coastline began to attract tourists in the 1960s, Málaga has acted as a gateway to the area's beaches thanks to its international airport. More recently, after investments in infrastructure and plans to attract technology firms, Málaga is emerging as a cultural destination and economic hub to rival Madrid, Barcelona and Valencia.

Citigroup has an office steps away from the 16th-century cathedral, and Google is planning to open a cybersecurity centre on the seafront. Following the launch of the Technology Park of Andalucía in 1992, companies have helped foster a global community of young professionals that has brought vitality to one of Spain's oldest cities. Expats with children can choose from French, German and British schools, while the Málaga-Costa del Sol Airport and the high-speed train station provide vital transport links.

SPAIN

RESIDENCE
CITY APARTMENT
Madrid

Spain offers everything from island boltholes, rural hideaways and inner-city apartments to choose from. We peek inside three properties to get some inspiration – first up, a light-filled apartment in Madrid.

One of the first things *Manera* magazine editor Enric Pastor did when he renovated his Madrid apartment was remove a number of walls from the common areas. "I love large and airy spaces," he says. He took on the project in 2020 with the help of Cano Estudio interior design. The L-shaped apartment occupies an enviable corner in the Lavapiés neighbourhood, with eight balconies overlooking an old square. Pastor paired light grey walls with pops of colour dotted throughout the home, including a Hay indigo-blue sofa and yellow floor lamp by Studio Job for Moooi. "I love colour very much, but sometimes I have to contain myself," he says. As the former editor in chief of interior design magazine *Architectural Digest España,* he has plenty of inspiration at his fingertips, but Pastor and his partner favour a minimalist and functional look. "The space is like a habitable tetris, each piece of furniture is positioned where it can be used and not just where it looks pretty."

RESIDENCE
RURAL RENOVATION
Olives, Galicia

Forgotten areas of rural Spain are being rediscovered, with a wealth of dilapidated buildings ripe for renovation. This charming rectory near Santiago de Compostela has been respectfully reimagined as a contemporary home.

The rolling hillsides of northern Spain are dotted with *hórreos* (granaries from the 15th century) while hamlets seem to spring out of the landscape. These small rural communities have been dwindling over the past century: 95.9 per cent of Spain's population is concentrated in the country's cities and coastal regions. This has left entire villages empty, buildings left to ruin. In Galicia an 18th-century rectory, uninhabited for 40 years, provided an opportunity for María José Alasa and Alejandro Valladares Durán to transform a forgotten residence into a cherished home. When the couple purchased the house, sections of the roof had collapsed and sheep sheltered on the ground floor. "We wanted to create a home that is warm and contemporary," says Alasa. Architect José Valladares Durán (Alejandro's brother) preserved the stone walls while a skylight was installed above the triple-height hallway, offering a glimpse of the original bell-gable that extends up beyond the roof. The restoration expertly balances the building's history with a design for modern living.

SPAIN

RESIDENCE
HOLIDAY HOME
Formentera

Spain offers plenty in the way of beachside retreats. A traditional white-washed villa on the tiny island of Formentera provides a welcome escape for one Madrileño couple.

Writer Ana García-Siñeriz and her husband Gauthier Peyrouzet bought this house in Formentera in 2010 after holidaying on the island for many years. The pair now travel from their main residence in Madrid almost every month. "We're completely insulated from everything here; from the world, from its noise," García-Siñeriz says. Formentera's population is a mere 12,000 and there is just one highway. "Everything takes place on a more human scale on a small island," she says. "Arriving back puts you in a different state." The house has thick walls with small inset windows, typical of the island vernacular. Large retractable doors at each end of the kitchen channel the sea breeze through the L-shaped layout, while allowing the seamless flow of movement between the cooking area and outdoor terrace. Earthy tones from baskets and *esparto*-woven rugs, linen curtains, and brick-coloured floor tiles, are in keeping with the island's function-over-fashion feel. "People must adapt to life here," says García-Siñeriz. "They must learn to go with the flow."

Whether you want to build a home, launch a business or even open a hotel, these are the trusted contacts to call for your next project.

ARCHITECTURE & DESIGN

ARCHITECTURE STUDIO
OHLAB
Mallorca

Architecture firm Ohlab is run by husband-and-wife team Jaime Oliver and Paloma Hernaiz. It has made a name for itself by designing buildings that sit at ease with their environment, limit the need for air-conditioning and heating, and use tactile materials and muted colour palettes in extraordinary ways. The firm was based in Madrid but the duo found themselves commuting to Mallorca with such regularity that they decided to flip: Palma became the HQ and they could jump on a plane to the capital when needed. Ohlab has designed everything from sleek apartment blocks and holiday homes to Palma's Can Bordoy hotel (*see page 36*). *ohlab.net*

ARCHITECTURE STUDIO
JEREZ ARQUITECTOS
Burgos, Castilla y León

ARCHITECTURE STUDIO
GCA ARCHITECTS
Barcelona

GCA Architects are behind some of the most striking additions to Barcelona's skyline. There's the 22-storey Puig Tower (in collaboration with Rafael Moneo), gleaming Diagrame office building and beachfront Seatowers building – all combining contemporary design with the highest eco-efficiency standards. The practice was founded in 1986 by Josep Juanpere and Antonio Puig and has become one of Spain's leading studios. Today it specialises in large-scale commercial projects from office buildings to luxury hotels. "Our architectural concept is in constant evolution," says Juanpere. "We stick to the context and generate long-term value."
gcaarchitects.com

When Jerez Arquitectos was approached in 2018 to design the Cobo Estratos restaurant in the centre of Burgos, it was apprehensive – many of the studio's initial projects were geared towards private residences and interior design. Cobo was the studio's first restaurant and required a different approach: it was to be three floors and mostly underground. "We needed to open up the space and introduce more natural light," says founder Enrique Jerez Abajo. The firm has since become a go-to for restaurant design in the area.
jerezarquitectos.com

DESIGN STUDIO
CASA JOSEPHINE
Madrid

Iñigo Aragón and Pablo López Navarro met whilst at university and between them hold degrees in art history, fashion design and photography – disciplines which visibly shape their current work. The duo's first project together was a guesthouse in La Rioja (*see page 27*) and their Madrid-based studio Casa Josephine has since designed a suite of inviting residential and commercial spaces across the country. The pair also run a vintage furniture and art showroom in the city's Rastro neighbourhood, a newer rental property near Segovia furnished in their signature style and have launched their own furniture and lighting range.
casajosephine.com

LIGHTING
CONTAIN
Mallorca

Originally from Argentina, Mauricio Obarrio and Juan Peralta run their lighting and furniture company from Palma. Their lamps are stunning – from alabaster and brass pendants to modular chandeliers and 1950s-inspired floor lights – and their way of doing business is key to their progress. "We sell direct but we are not an e-com site," says Peralta. "There are no prices on the website. It's very personalised and you have to contact us to place an order." Obarrio explains: "We give people a customised product – they are creating the product with us." Customers can select colours, materials and finishes for a truly bespoke solution.
contain.es

TILES
HUGUET
Mallorca

Biel Huguet's grandfather founded Huguet in 1933, running a thriving business making colourful floor tiles. By the time Biel's father inherited it in the 1970s, the world had changed and old crafts were being sidelined. After his father died suddenly, Biel (*pictured*) found himself at the helm of a company in disarray. He looked to the past for inspiration and started remaking the colourful floor tiles that had given Huguet its first success, recognising that people moving to Mallorca were restoring old houses. Today, the company has collaborated with Herzog & de Meuron, David Chipperfield and Pentagram's designers, among others.
huguetmallorca.com

SPAIN

Searching for the perfect pieces to furnish your new home or venture? Look no further – we highlight a Basque brand, a Madrid shop stacked with vintage gems and a Barcelona instution with all the classics.

FURNITURE

FURNITURE BRAND
TREKU
Zarautz, Basque Country

In 1947 Jesús Aldabaldetreku opened a workshop in Zarautz and called it Treku, an abbreviation of his surname. Treku soon grew into a profitable furniture factory but after the 2008 financial crisis Aldabaldetreku's grandsons Gorka and Xabier overhauled the company's style in a bid to attract international buyers. "We had to present something that people in Frankfurt or Paris hadn't seen," Gorka says. Today, the company's design is understated but it possesses a distinct flair, whether in pointed cabinet legs or an unexpected pop of yellow. "It is not Italian or Scandinavian. It's Basque."
treku.com

FURNITURE SHOP
IKB191
Madrid

"This shop is a living exhibition," says Nicolás Poggetti, manager of the eclectic shop and interior design studio. IKB191 is named after French artist Yves Klein's patented colour International Klein Blue, and stocks mid-century furniture and lighting as well as contemporary artwork, chiefly by emerging artists. Also for sale are limited-edition collaborations with Spanish designers. In 2021, founders Carlos and Rubén López, third generation antiquarians, moved the business from Madrid's open-air market El Rastro to Chueca. IKB191 resists aesthetic trends, presenting a case for the rediscovery of pieces that have previously been overlooked.
ikb191.es

FURNITURE SHOP
CUBIÑÁ
Barcelona

The Cubiñá family has been selling furniture for more than a century. In 2006, it made the decision to focus on high-end contemporary wares and moved into a space within the historic Casa Thomas. The building dates back to the late 1800s and is the work of architect Lluís Domènech i Montaner, who also designed the city's Palau de la Música Catalana concert hall (*see page 138*). Its carved wooden panelling and painted ceilings provide an impressive backdrop for an array of furniture and homeware from the likes of Artemide and Pedrali. There are also homegrown names, including lighting brand Marset and Nanimarquina rugs (*see page 87*).
cubinya.es

One of Spain's biggest draws is its strong sense of community –
but how do you build your own? Consider joining a club,
be it for tennis, yachts or simply socialising.

BUILD A NETWORK

MEMBER'S CLUB
CLUB MATADOR
Madrid

In Madrid's upmarket Salamanca neighbourhood you'll find Club Matador, which was founded in 2013 by the team behind *Matador* magazine. The private club offers members a ready-made community comprising the best of the city's powerful and well-connected – and in a rather beautiful setting. The elegant building houses multiple cocktail bars and restaurants that vary from casual to fine dining. A well-stocked library provides a place for reflection, while an old-school smoking room offers quite the opposite: a space for deliciously clandestine conversations. There's also a theatre that plays host to an impressive cultural agenda.
clubmatador.com

SPORT CLUB
PALMA SPORT & TENNIS CLUB
Mallorca

Based around Francesc Mitjans' 1960s low-slung, lattice-concrete clubhouse, the Palma Sport & Tennis Club has been a favourite haunt of the smart set since its conception. Today the club, which was refurbished in 2015, is beautiful but means business: the five clay courts are for playing (they host the ATP Legends Cup); the gym is photogenic but designed for making members more so; and the pool – though it shimmers like a Hockney – is for lengths. But it's not all work: the spa is a place to indulge while the bistro is the perfect spot for a post-match debrief with new friends – and going the full five sets makes a chilled glass of *albariño* that much crisper.
palmatennis.com

YACHT CLUB
CLUB MARÍTIMO DE CANIDO
Vigo, Galicia

With more than 1,500km of coastline (almost 20 per cent of Spain's total) pocked with inlets and dotted with pretty fishing villages, it will come as no surprise that Galicia is home to many sailing and yacht clubs. Most – like Club Marítimo Canido on the outskirts of Vigo – have become anchors of the community and are multi-generational spaces where members come to socialise as much as head out on the water. This club, which was founded in 1969, is open year-round and offers both beginner sailing lessons and more advanced courses for those looking to perfect their technique, plus a restaurant with views of the Islas Cíes (*see page 163*).
cmcanido.es

SPAIN

You know where to move to, the contacts to call on, plus what your home could look like – it's time to hear from the expats who chose the country as a home for their new ventures.

SUCCESS STORIES

DESIGNER
ANNA LENA KORTMANN
Studio Jaia, Mallorca

Anna Lena Kortmann grew up in Cairo, studied in Mainz, Melbourne and Paris, and became an interior architecture and exhibition designer in Los Angeles and Berlin. But she was after something – and somewhere – else. She knew Mallorca from holidays and started spending time on the island. "I discovered these traditional chairs with beautiful weaving," says Kortmann. "I found someone who taught me how to do the craft. It was not a business idea to start with but it became one." Kortmann started her firm in 2019 and now has a shop-cum-atelier in Palma, making everything herself, including tapping into her woodworking skills.
studiojaia.com

CAFÉ OWNER
VICKY GROSSO IGARZABAL
Fran Café, Valencia

GALLERISTS
CHRISTIAN BOURDAIS & EVA ALBARRÁN
Albarrán Bourdais, Madrid

Quality of life, a sense of community and a familial culture: just three reasons why Vicky Grosso Igarzabal decided to make Valencia her new home. Leaving unrest behind in her native Argentina, Igarzabal moved to Spain and opened Fran Café (the name an homage to her hometown, where the Franca Austral whale migrates in the winter) in the city's Ruzafa neighbourhood in 2022. Starting out in the unknown had its challenges. "I knew nothing of Spain's bureaucracy, what kind of permits I needed or how long everything would take," she says. But both Igarzabal and the café have been welcomed into the community: "So many people helped us out."
+34 610 121 155

Gallerists Christian Bourdais and Eva Albarrán are some of France's most important producers of contemporary art, who are now operating in Spain. The pair opened Galería Albarrán Bourdais in Madrid's lively Chueca area with the aim of offering artists a gateway to Spanish and Latin American markets. "We are interested in developing close relationships with our artists, as well as the collectors," says Bourdais. The pair have continued to invest in the country's cultural scene with Solo Houses, a one-of-a-kind, open-air museum (which will also feature a hotel and vineyard) located in the mountainous Matarranya region.
albarran-bourdais.com

PART 03

THE ADDRESS BOOK

A handy guide for planning your next visit
with our round up of the best places to stay,
eat, shop and see in each region.

MADRID

Spain's first city boasts everything from world-leading museums and avant-garde galleries to a wealth of luxury hotels to rest your head. Don't miss the vibrant gastronomic scene, which includes Michelin-starred restaurants, old-school Spanish bars and informal bistros.

STAY

GRAN HOTEL INGLÉS
Barrio de las Letras
Madrid's oldest hotel was formerly a speakeasy (*see page 29*).
granhotelingles.com

ROSEWOOD VILLA MAGNA
Chamberí
The perfect base to explore the city on foot with an exceptional in-house restaurant, Amós (*see page 28*).
rosewoodhotels.com

SANTO MAURO
Chamberí
Built in 1902, this *casa palacio* is one of Madrid's most elegant hideaways.
marriott.com

URSO HOTEL & SPA
Chueca
Historical details make Urso as irresistible as its location between Chamberí, Chueca and Malasaña.
hotelurso.com

MANDARIN ORIENTAL RITZ
Retiro
A careful restoration has returned this storied hotel to its gilded glory.
mandarinoriental.com

FOUR SEASONS HOTEL MADRID
Sol
This hotel from the Four Seasons is a masterclass in luxury hospitality.
fourseasons.com/madrid

THE MADRID EDITION
Sol
This design hotel boasts a rooftop pool and terrace bar (*see page 29*).
editionhotels.com/madrid

EAT & DRINK

FORMAJE
Almagro
Upmarket cheese shop selling the best Spanish produce (*see page 84*).
formaje.com

Parque del Buen Retiro boating lake

BARDERO
Arganzuela
An informal restaurant with an international-inspired menu.
bardero.es

BODEGAS ROSELL
Arganzuela
This traditional tavern opened in 1920 and boasts an extensive list of regional wines.
bodegasrosell.es

FISMULER
Chamberí
An upmarket restaurant serving a mix of Basque and Nordic fare.
fismuler.com

MERCADO DE VALLEHERMOSO
Chamberí
Casual market with more than 170 stalls selling everything from fruit and veg to street food (*see page 80*).
mercadovallehermoso.es

MERCATO BALLARÓ
Chamberí
This seafood restaurant was named after a market in Palermo.
mercatoballaro.com

LA PARRA
Chamberí
Old-school classic serving a mix of Spanish and English fare (*see page 53*).
restaurante-laparra.com

QUIMBAYA
Chamberí
This Michelin-star restaurant offers modern Colombian cuisine.
quimbayarestaurant.com

LA DUQUESITA
Chueca
A luxurious bakery with a beautiful tea room (*see page 64*).
laduquesita.es

NATIF
Chueca
This coffee and brunch spot is perfect for late risers.
natif.es

TONI2
Chueca
A popular piano bar that only gets going past midnight.
toni2.es

TOMA CAFÉ
Conde Duce
Pint-sized speciality coffee shop popular with locals (*see page 68*).
toma.cafe

BAR COCK
Justicia
An old-school cocktail bar favoured by Madrid's journalists (*see page 75*).
+34 915 322 826

GOTA
Justicia
This futuristic bar pairs natural wines with a rotating menu of simple fare (*see page 74*).
gotawine.es

GRAN CAFÉ SANTANDER
Justicia
This grand café serves a delectably soft *tortilla* (*see page 66*).
grancafesantander.com

JOSEFITA
Justicia
Head to this cosy bistro for hearty Andalucian dishes (*see page 53*).
josefitabar.es

EL BROTE
La Latina
An informal bistro run by expert mushroom foragers.
elbrote.es

LOS CHUCHIS BAR
Lavapiés
A popular neighbourhood joint serving modern tapas. Book ahead.
+34 911 276 606

SAVAS
Lavapiés
This bar serves some of the country's best cocktails (*see page 74*).
Calle de la Sombrerería 3

CASA FIDEL
Malasaña
A rare gem featuring a menu full of Madrid's most traditional dishes.
+34 915 317 736

LA COLMADA
Malasaña
Sample delicious tinned treats at this eclectic royal-blue-hued bar.
lacolmada.com

IKIGAI VELÁZQUEZ
Salamanca
Dine here for an impressive fusion of Spanish and Japanese cuisines.
ikigairestaurantes.com

DANI BRASSERIE
Sol
An upmarket rooftop bar at the top of the Four Seasons (*see page 73*).
danibrasserie.com

LHARDY
Sol
One of the oldest restaurants in Madrid, this storied spot was supposedly a favourite of Queen Isabella II (*see page 52*).
lhardy.com

Wrought-iron balconies in the city

ALMA NOMAD
Trafalgar
Sample delicious baked goods at this popular spot (*see page 63*).
+34 613 026 888

SHOP

COCOL
Barrio de la Latina
This shop stocks handmade pieces from across Spain (*see page 98*).
cocolmadrid.es

TADO
Barrio de las Letras
A boutique specialising in ceramics crafted by homegrown artisans.
tado-pottery-store.negocio.site

OLAVIDE BAR DE LIBROS
Chamberí
Enjoy a coffee or a glass of wine with a novel at this bar-cum-bookshop.
olavidelibros.com

IKB191
Chueca
Furniture store filled with mid-century gems (*see page 191*).
ikb191.es

MISIA
Conde Duque
Womenswear boutique popular with Madrid's discerning fashion crowd.
misiamadrid.com

LA FÁBRICA
Huertas
A contemporary bookshop with an exhibition and design space.
tienda.lafabrica.com

CASA GONZÁLEZ & GONZÁLEZ
Justicia
Small homeware shop with an onus on the handmade (*see page 113*).
gonzalez-gonzalez.es

ECOALF
Justicia
Sustainable clothing brand with a mission to clean up the world's oceans (*see page 105*).
ecoalf.com

EL RASTRO
La Latina
A popular open-air Sunday market that's been running since 1740.
Calle de la Ribera de Curtidores 5

OTEYZA
Las Salesas
Head here for handmade suits and expert tailoring (*see page 104*).
deoteyza.com

PEZ
Las Salesas
A well-appointed multibrand womenswear store (*see page 98*).
pez-pez.es

GARCIA MADRID
Malasaña
This menswear store is famed for its classic tailoring with a twist.
garciamadrid.com

JAVIER S MEDINA CARPINTERIA 28
Malasaña
Visit this shop-cum-atelier for unique woven works (*see page 96*).
javiersmedina.com

MAGRO CARDONA
Malasaña
Women's footwear that fuses the traditional and the modern.
magrocardona.com

LE SECRET DU MARAIS
Malasaña
Perfumery known for niche scents.
lesecretdumarais.com

SPORTIVO
Malasaña
Sportivo sells more than 60 global menswear brands (*see page 103*).
sportivostore.com

LLOP MADRID
Paseo del Arte
Concept shop stocking Spanish wares and clothing (*see page 101*).
llopmadrid.com

GLENT
Salamanca
Stop here for upmarket custom-made men's shoes (*see page 111*).
glentshoes.com

LOEWE
Salamanca
Visit the luxury fashion house's flagship shop in the city where it was founded (*see page 107*).
loewe.com

PEDRO GARCÍA
Salamanca
Footwear label that sells everything from sandals to clogs (*see page 111*).
pedrogarcia.com

CAPAS SESEÑA
Sol
In business since 1901, Capas Seseña is the place to buy a cape in Madrid from traditional silhouettes to modern iterations (*see page 107*).
sesena.com

CASA DE DIEGO
Sol
This shop offers a vibrant collection of hand-held fans (*see page 97*).
casadediego.info

Painting the town in Madrid

PAPERGROUND
Trafalgar
Magazine and bookshop stocking international titles (*see page 140*).
Calle de Medellín 4

DO

FUNDACIÓN MARÍA CRISTINA MASAVEU PETERSON
Chamberí
This cultural centre and art space is houses in a refurbished 20th-century *palacete* and features rotating exhibitions.
fundacioncristinamasaveu.com

MUSEO SOROLLA
Chamberí
Painter Joaquín Sorolla's former residence and studio.
culturaydeporte.gob.es/msorolla

ALBARRÁN BOURDAIS
Chueca
Commercial gallery by French-Spanish duo (*see page 193*).
albarran-bourdais.com

EL CHICO
La Latina
Compact gallery with a focus on emerging Spanish creatives.
elchico.net

SALA EQUIS
La Latina
Art-house cinema and bar showing films in their original languages.
salaequis.es

MUSEO REINA SOFÍA
Lavapiés
One of Madrid's best-known art museums (*see page 131*).
museoreinasofia.es

TABACALERA PROMOCIÓN DEL ARTE
Lavapiés
Former tobacco factory-turned-gallery featuring contemporary art.
promociondelarte.com/tabacalera

ESPACIO VALVERDE
Malasaña
Multidisciplinary gallery run by a Madrileño couple (*see page 137*).
espaciovalverde.com

MICROTEATRO POR DINERO
Malasaña
A former brothel-turned-theatre known for its 15-minute-long plays.
microteatro.es

LA CASA ENCENDIDA
Ronda de Valencia
This cultural centre focuses on avant-garde art (*see page 134*).
lacasaencendida.es

CENTRAL

Head beyond the Spanish capital and discover the country's vast central regions with sleek countryside hotels, authentic restaurants and cultural institutions that are well worth the journey.

STAY

PARADOR DE CUENCA
Castilla La Mancha (Cuenca)
From the Paradores de Turismo group, this renowned hotel boasts breathtaking views.
paradores.es

PARADOR DE SEGOVIA
Castilla y León (Segovia)
Another by the Paradores group, this 1970s hotel is worth a visit for its architecture alone (see page 24).
parador.es

FUENTE ACEÑA HOTEL BOUTIQUE
Castilla y León (Valladolid)
An ideal base for those visiting nearby vineyards and *bodegas*.
fuenteacena.es

ABADÍA RETUERTA LEDOMAINE
Castilla y León (Valladolid)
A hotel and vineyard set in a former monastery. It boasts a number of impressive artworks and a Michelin-starred restaurant (see page 25).
abadia-retuerta.com

ATRIO
Extremadura (Cáceres)
Hotel and restaurant decorated with the owners' personal art collection – including a Warhol (see page 37).
restauranteatrio.com

EAT & DRINK

EL 51 DEL SOL
Castilla y León (Aranda del Duero)
This spot serves traditional Castilian dishes with contemporary flair.
el51delsol.com

RESTAURANTE PASAPÁN
Castilla y León (Segovia)
Informal restaurant serving hearty international dishes.
restaurantepasapan.es

View over the city of Segovia

SHOP

ÁBBATTE
Castilla y León (Segovia)
Run by a mother-and-daughter duo, this textiles brand is set in the ruins of a former monastery with a focus on all-natural products (see page 89).
abbatte.com

REAL FÁBRICA DE CRISTALES DE LA GRANJA
Castilla y León (Segovia)
This glass factory once supplied its wares to the palace.
realfabricadecristales.es

DO

FUNDACIÓN ANTONIO PÉREZ
Castilla La Mancha (Cuenca)
This centre hosts the personal collection of Antonio Pérez, best known as a found-object artist.
fundacionantonioperez.com

MUSEO DE ARTE ABSTRACTO ESPAÑOL
Castilla La Mancha (Cuenca)
Perched on the side of a gorge, this spectacular museum is home to works by Spain's key abstract artists.
march.es/cuenca

PEÑA TIERRA ARANDA
Castilla y León (Aranda del Duero)
Sip wine in a storied underground bodega (the city's wine cellars date from the 12th century).
tierraranda.com

ACUEDUCTO DE SEGOVIA
Castilla y León (Segovia)
This 30-metre-tall Roman aqueduct is a marvel of civil engineering built in the first century.
Plaza del Azoguejo

LA CÁRCEL – SEGOVIA CENTRO DE CREACIÓN
Castilla y León (Segovia)
A former jail, this gallery houses multidisciplinary art by local artists.
lacarceldesegovia.com

JARDINES DEL PALACIO REAL DE LA GRANJA
Castilla y León (Segovia)
Royal gardens featuring 21 large-scale ornamental fountains.
patrimonionacional.es

MUSEO DE ARTE CONTEMPORÁNEO HELGA DE ALVEAR
Extremadura (Cáceres)
Visit for the contemporary art collection donated by the German-born gallerist (see page 131).
museohelgadealvear.com

BARCELONA

Explore Barna – as this popular city is known by those in the know – and all it has to offer, from well-stocked independent shops, forward-thinking galleries and first-rate restaurants.

STAY

MERCER HOTEL BARCELONA
Barri Gòtic
This 28-room hotel offers five-star luxury and an excellent restaurant.
mercerbarcelona.com

YURBBAN TRAFALGAR
El Born
Centrally-located hotel with plush rooms, a rooftop pool and spa.
yurbbantrafalgar.com

CASA BONAY
Eixample
This townhouse overlooking Gran Vía tempts a creative crowd class negronis and DJ sets (see page 31).
casabonay.com

COTTON HOUSE
Eixample
A 19th-century mansion with a rooftop pool and great views across the neighbourhood (see page 30).
hotelcottonhouse.com

HOTEL PULITZER
Eixample
The hotel's interiors come courtesy of designer Lázaro Rosa-Violán and attract a particularly dapper crowd.
hotelpulitzer.es

HOTEL BRUMMELL
Poble Sec
Contemporary hotel with industrial interiors overlooking Montjuïc.
hotelbrummell.com

EAT & DRINK

FISKEBAR
Barceloneta
Restaurant in one of the city's oldest yacht clubs serving seafood with a Nordic and Mediterranean focus.
grupotragaluz.com

Interior of Gaudí's Sagrada Familia

BALDOMERO
Eixample
This spot serves brunch buffet-style on the weekends (see page 42).
casabaldomero.com

BAR CUGAT
Eixample
A refined bar open for breakfast that serves tapas into the evening.
barcugat.com

CLOUDSTREET BAKERY
Eixample
This bakery (which has a second site in Sant Martí) makes the best *coca de forner* flatbreads in town (see page 62).
cloudstreet.es

LA DAMA
Eixample
Fine-dining institution heavy on old-school charm and housed within modernista mansion Casa Sayrach.
la-dama.com

EROICA CAFFÈ
Eixample
Bike-themed café serving fresh pasta and coffee. There's also a cycling club and bike workshop.
eroica.cc

FUNKY BAKERS EATERY
Eixample
Middle Eastern-inspired restaurant with dishes such as za'atar-marinated lamb and halloumi.
funkybakers.com

GRANJA VENDRELL
Eixample
An iconic bistro that offers a mix of Catalan classics and has an art-deco interior (see page 44).
+34 930 112 150

GRESCA
Eixample
This tapas spot, run by former El Bulli chef, is raising Catalan cuisine to new heights (see page 41).
gresca.rest

PARKING PIZZA
Eixample
This former car park is now a stylish pizza place with communal tables.
parkingpizza.com

BAR BRUTAL
El Born
Wine bar run by an Italian sommelier and his chef brother.
barbrutal.com

JONCAKE
El Born
A bakery known for its cheesecakes and their inventive flavours.
joncake.es

NOMAD COFFEE
El Born
A speciality coffee shop near to the Cathedral of Barcelona (see page 68).
nomadcoffee.es

BALIUS
El Poblenou
Lively bar in a former pharmacy hosting live jazz on Sundays.
baliusbar.com

CAMPING
El Poblenou
Kiosk in the Parc del Poblenou serving beers, *tortilla* and *bocadillos*.
campingcamping.onuniverse.com

ORVAL
Fort Pienc
Sunny coffee spot near Parc de La Ciutadella that also sells magazines.
Carrer de Buenaventura Muñoz 31

EL PUESTU
Fort Pienc
Bar serving classic tapas with a twist, including baked snails with aioli.
elpuestu.com

THREE MARKS COFFEE
Fort Pienc
Speciality roasters with three locations across Barcelona. The Fort Pienc outpost is our favourite.
threemarkscoffee.com

COUSH ARMÓ
Gràcia
Baker Francisco Seubert prepares dishes from his native Argentina.
Carrer de San Marc 19

FONDA PEPA
Gràcia
Old-school bistro plating up refined but hearty local dishes (see page 43).
fondapepa.com

SOMODÓ
Gràcia
Fine-dining restaurant with a Mediterranean-Japanese menu.
somodo.es

XEMEI
Poble Sec
Restaurant known for its big portions of Venetian cuisine.
xemei.es

PINHAN
Sarrià-Sant Gervasi
Coffees, pastries and light lunches are available at this casual kiosk in the city's Parc del Turó.
pinhan.es

La Gamba by Javier Mariscal

SHOP

BRUTUS DE GAPER
Bogatell
This vast warehouse from Niels Jansen and Ron Van Melick is filled with vintage furniture and colourful homewares.
brutusdegaper.com

CUBIÑA
Eixample
Contemporary furniture and homewares shop (see page 189).
cubinya.es

LES EINES
Eixample
Interior design store with a selection of contemporary and vintage furnishings.
leseines.com

LLIBRERIA FINESTRES
Eixample
Inviting bookshop that hosts regular readings from visiting authors.
llibreriafinestres.com

NANIMARQUINA
Eixample
This textile brand's rugs feature pops of colour and contemporary design elements (see page 87).
nanimarquina.com

SANTA EULALIA
Eixample
Multibrand store that's occupied the same luxurious premises on Passeig de Gràcia since 1944.
santaeulalia.com

SHON MOTT
Eixample
Family-run clothing brand creating minimalist men's and women's lines.
shonmott.com

APRÈS SKI
El Born
Lucía Vergara's jewellery brand focuses on delicate handmade designs with a folksy touch.
apresski.es

CHANDAL
El Born
Small concept shop selling everything from magazines and homeware to analogue cameras.
chandal.tv

WORKING IN THE REDWOODS
El Born
Ceramicist Miriam Cernuda makes earth-toned vases, plates and bowls in the workshop adjoining the shop.
workingintheredwoods.com

HEREU
El Parc i la Llacuna del Poblenou
This shoe and handbag brand's owners met while working at fashion behemoth Inditex (see page 110).
hereustudio.com

HEYSHOP
El Raval
The shop where graphic design studio Hey sells its colourful wares.
heyshop.es

SANTA & COLE
La Roca del Vallès
Catalan lighting icon Santa & Cole is known for selling previously discontinued products (see page 90).
santacole.com

LIBRERÍA TERRANOVA
Sant Antoni
A former shoe shop that is now a bookshop and gallery (see page 141).
terrranova.com

BASSAL
Sarrià-Sant Gervasi
Bassal specialises in Spanish-designed clothing for men and women (see page 103).
bassal.store

DO

MUSEU DEL DISSENY
Bogatell
Four-storey museum spanning graphic, product and fashion design from the third century to the present day.
museudeldisseny.cat

PALAU DE LA MÚSICA CATALANA
El Born
This ornate concert hall was built in the 1900s and still presents classical and contemporary music to locals and visitors (see page 138).
palaumusica.cat

MUSEU CAN FRAMIS
El Poblenou
Museum that champions Catalan art from the 1960s onwards (see page 130).
fundaciovilacasas.com

LA NAU
El Poblenou
Live music venue with an impressive programme of international acts.
lanaubarcelona.es

Bar Bodega Quimet in Gràcia

CENTRE DE CULTURA CONTEMPORÀNIA DE BARCELONA
El Raval
Multidisciplinary institution hosting exhibitions that explore cultural, scientific and historical phenomena.
cccb.org

MACBA
El Raval
The city's main museum of modern art has an array of some 5,000 works.
macba.cat

CASA VICENS
Gràcia
This museum was Gaudí's first residential project (see page 146).
casavicens.org

RECINTE MODERNISTA DE SANT PAU
Guinardó
This former hospital is now a museum and architectural landmark.
santpaubarcelona.org

MNAC
Montjuïc
A museum that explores Catalan art history from medieval to modern.
museunacional.cat

FUNDACIÓ JOAN MIRÓ
Parc de Montjuïc
Gallery dedicated to homegrown artist Joan Miró (see page 125).
fmirobcn.org

PHENOMENA
Poblet
Single-screen cinema showing independent films and cult classics alongside new releases.
phenomena-experience.com

MUSEU PICASSO
Ribera
This museum hosts 4,000 works by the famed artist from the early years of his career (see page 127).
museupicasso.bcn.cat

ALZUETA
Sèneca
This contemporary gallery is set in a former textiles factory (see page 137).
alzuetagallery.com

CATALUÑA

Cataluña distinctly differs from the rest of Spain – it has its own language and unique customs, for instance. Catalans are fiercely proud of their region too and it's clear to see why with its medieval towns, Costa Brava coast and mountainous landscapes.

STAY

LA BIONDA
Begur
Eight-room hotel filled with a playful mix of vintage and bespoke furnishings (see page 18).
labiondabegur.com

CASA NERETA
Cadaqués
The home of painter Joan Ponç is now a charming hotel (see page 17).
casanereta.com

VIU EMPORDÀ
Costa Brava
A string of 11 historic farmhouses that can be rented.
viuemporda.com

PARADOR D'AIGUABLAVA
Costa Brava
Clifftop hotel perched high above a rocky cove with exceptional views.
paradores.es

ALEMANYS 5
Girona
Sixteenth-century house converted into two sleek holiday apartments.
alemanys5.com

CASA BOUMORT
Lleida
Small hotel with stylish mid-century furnishings nestled amid the scenic foothills of the Pyrenees.
casaboumort.com

OLLER DEL MAS
Manresa
This winery has 22 wooden cabins with views of Montserrat.
ollerdelmas.com

EAT & DRINK

COMPARTIR
Cadaqués
Chef Marc Llach serves modern sharing dishes at this refined spot.
compartircadaques.com

Scorpion fish in Cadaqués

MARGARITA
Costa Brava
Pint-sized beachfront bistro serving seafood dishes such as prawn ceviche and lobster rolls.
margarita-calella.com

CAFÉ LE BISTROT
Girona
A quaint restaurant with views of Església de Sant Martí Sacosta.
lebistrot.cat

NORMAL
Girona
The famed Roca Brothers are behind this pared-back spot (see page 45).
cellercanroca.com

BÀRBARA FORÉS
Tarragona
Family-run vineyard known for its wines made using traditional and organic methods (see page 70).
cellerbarbarafores.com

SHOP

CASTAÑER
Banyoles
A storied espadrille brand that's been making the traditional Spanish footwear since 1927 (see page 110).
castaner.com

ROSA CADAQUÉS
Cadaqués
This florist specialises in dried flower bouquets for every occasion and season.
rosacadaques.com

ÚLTIMA PARADA
Corçà
Choose from an eclectic mix of vintage furnishings at this vast emporium – complete with a modern greenery-filled restaurant.
ultima-parada.com

DO

CASA MUSEO SALVADOR DALÍ
Portlligat
The former home of Salvador Dalí has been preserved by the artist's foundation. The museum, which resembles a cabinet of curiosities, has been open to the public since 1997 (see page 123).
salvador-dali.org

VALENCIA

While many overlook Valencia in favour of Madrid and Barcelona, a savvy crowd is fast realising its potential. Let us introduce you to Spain's third city – including the old-school paella joints, designers to know and cultural institutions you must not miss.

STAY

PALACIO VALLIER
La Seu
This hotel is a glitzy affair in a 19th-century mansion, once home to a Roman perfumery.
myrhotels.com

ONLY YOU HOTEL
La Xerea
Set in Valencia's historic old town, this five star hotel was designed by Barcelona's Lázaro Rosa-Violán.
onlyyouhotels.com

YOURS BOUTIQUE HOTEL
Ruzafa
A homely 12-room hotel with contemporary interiors and a tropical terrace complete with a lap pool (see page 32).
thisisyours.es

EAT & DRINK

CHIRINGUITO EL OCHO
Alboraya
Informal beach bar at the far end of Valencia's sandy stretch that serves excellent tapas and drinks.
+34 634 839 961

LA PLAYA DE MODA
Alboraya
On Patacona beach, La Playa de Moda serves tasty Valencian cuisine – you can also order food and drinks to your sunlounger (see page 46).
laplayademoda.com

GRAN MARTÍNEZ
Bajo
Gran Martínez is an elegant, wood-panelled bar with an enviable cocktail menu (see page 77).
granmartinez.com

LA FÁBRICA DE HIELO
El Cabanyal
This former ice factory is now a lively beach-side cultural hub.
lafabricadehielo.net

Dishing out paella in Valencia

LA PEPICA
El Cabanyal
A classic paella restaurant from 1898 that's heralded as one of Valencia's best (see page 45).
lapepica.com

LA SASTRERÍA
El Cabanyal
With an eclectic tiled-interior, this colourful bistro and bar dishing up innovative Mediterranean fare with a creative cocktail offering.
lasastreriavalencia.com

MERCABANYAL
El Cabanyal
Outdoor street-food market serving everything from bao buns to tapas.
mercabanyal.com

VINOSTRUM
El Carmen
Cosy wine bar offering a selection of tipples and traditional tapas.
+34 691 849 076

MERCADO CENTRAL DE VALENCIA
El Mercat
This market houses some 1,200 retailers. Stop at Central Bar for award-winning tapas when you've finished shopping (see page 81).
Plaça de la Ciutat de Bruges

PALANCA CARNISSERS
El Mercat
A family-run butchery based in the city's Mercado Central de Valencia (see page 85).
palancacarnissers.com

MÒLT BAKERY
La Gran Via
Gonzalo Pertusa, who cut his culinary teeth in San Sebastián and Bordeaux, crafts his bread from regional ingredients.
moltdepa.es

CASA CARMELA
La Malvarrosa
Another local favourite, Casa Carmela's bestsellers include its lobster and langoustine paellas.
casa-carmela.com

FEDERAL
La Xerea
An Australia-inspired brunch spot that's popular with locals. Think smashed avocado, fluffy pancakes and flat whites.
federalcafe.es/valencia

OSTRAS PEDRÍN
La Xerea
This utilitarian bar serves some of the best oysters in town (see page 46).
ostraspedrin.es

VACHATA
Ruzafa
Traditional *horchata*, a sweet and milky Valencian delicacy, is made at this modern spot (see page 64).
+34 640 175 342

NOZOMI
Ruzafa
Elegant sushi bar taking advantage of the city's seafood bounty.
nozomisushibar.es

BLUEBELL COFFEE
Ruzafa
The coffee connoisseurs at Bluebell Coffee offer tasty seasonal roasts.
bluebellcoffeeco.com

FRAN CAFÉ
Ruzafa
A welcoming speciality coffee shop in a trendy spot (see page 193).
+34 610 121 155

SHOP

SEBASTIAN MELMOTH
El Carmen
This concept shop, named after Oscar Wilde's book, stocks everything from Japanese ceramics to Armenian paper.
sebastianmelmothstore.com

ABSOLUTA FLORA
El Pilar
Florist that also offers ceramics, homewares and houseplants.
absolutaflora.com

CANDELA EN RAMA
El Pilar
Minimal Mediterranean-inspired jewellery that's crafted and sold at this elegant shop (see page 99).
candelaenrama.com

EDIT 32
Sant Francesc
Multibrand clothing store offering luxury womenswear.
edit32store.com

POPPYNS
Sant Francesc
Poppyns is a favourite among Valencia's best-dressed, selling homegrown and global labels.
poppyns.com

Play time on La Malvarrosa beach

CANOA LAB
Ruzafa
Canoa Lab's ceramics are crafted using a number of techniques. The result is its selection of sophisticated one-of-a-kind pieces (see page 92).
canoalab.com

DO

CCCC
El Carmen
The Centro del Carmen de Cultura Contemporánea (CCCC) is a cultural centre set in a 13th-century convent. It's worth a visit to see the historic cloisters and clock tower.
consorcimuseus.gva.es

IVAM
El Carmen
The Institut Valencià d'Art Modern was Spain's first modern art museum and remains one of the country's key cultural players.
ivam.es

GALERÍA ROSA SANTOS
El Pilar
This modern exhibition space is run by one of the city's most prominent female gallerists.
rosasantos.net

GALERÍA VANGAR
La Gran Via
Exciting spot championing mid-career Valencian artists.
galeriavangar.com

LUIS ADELANTADO
La Xerea
Commercial art gallery promoting homegrown and international contemporary artists.
luisadelantadovlc.com

BOMBAS GENS
Marxalenes
This old industrial complex is now a cultural centre that boasts an art gallery, Michelin-starred restaurant and peaceful garden.
bombasgens.com

CIUDAD DE LAS ARTES Y LAS CIENCIAS
Quatre Carreres
The gargantuan cultural and architectural attraction contains an IMAX theatre, CaixaForum and science museum, as well as an opera house (see page 147).
cac.es

JARDÍ DEL TURIA
Valencia
The former riverbed of the Río Turia was converted into the city's green lung in the 1980s in a drastic urban planning project.

THE EAST

The country's east, aka the Costa Blanca, has become known across Europe for its holiday resorts – namely Benidorm. But there are plenty of pockets that are yet to be discovered: including swathes of beaches, an unexpected art scene and a growing generation of creatives.

STAY

HOSPES AMÉRIGO
Valencia (Alicante)
This city-centre hotel boasts a rooftop pool and terrace with views across the Mediterranean and Santa Bárbara Castle.
hospes.com

HOTEL SERAWA
Valencia (Alicante)
Just 300 metres from Postiguet beach, this eco-conscious hotel incorporates Alicante's ancient city wall (*see page 39*).
serawahotels.com

EUROSTARS PÓRTICO ALICANTE
Valencia (Alicante)
Elegant hotel in the historic part of the city, with a roof terrace and bar.
eurostarshotels.com

NOMAD HOTEL XÁBIA PORT
Valencia (Jávea)
This intimate Moroccan-inspired hotel sits on the seafront, moments from the Playa de la Grava.
nomadhotelcollection.com

VILLA RIU BLANC
Valencia (Jávea)
A vibrant five-suite guesthouse on a verdant hilltop with views out to the Mediterranean (*see page 25*).
villariublanc.es

EAT & DRINK

BOCA DE VIN
Valencia (Alicante)
This little spot in the historical centre serves exceptional tapas and famously good baked bread.
+34 637 693 289

Salzillo restaurant in Murcia

LA TABERNA DEL GOURMET
Valencia (Alicante)
Open since 1979, this rustic tavern dishes up award-winning tapas.
latabernadelgourmet.com

XIRINGUITO POSTIGUET
Valencia (Alicante)
A beach bar offering cocktails and informal fare.
+34 654 016 573

LES FRESES
Valencia (Jesús Pobre)
This winery's grapes are grown on land that previously produced strawberries – hence the name.
lesfreses.com

GRAN RHIN BAR
Murcia (Murcia)
A great aperitif spot with excellent seafood dishes.
+34 652 165 401

MERCADO DE CORREOS
Murcia (Murcia)
Sleek food hall with everything from fine dining to tasty burgers.
mercadodecorreos.com

SALZILLO
Murcia (Murcia)
An old-school family-run bistro with a menu peppered with high-quality regional produce (*see page 47*).
restaurantesalzillo.com

DO

MACA
Valencia (Alicante)
Housed in a former 17th-century palace, this light-filled modern art museum hosts some 800 20th-century artworks.
maca-alicante.es

GALERÍA T20
Murcia (Murcia)
Contemporary art gallery championing homegrown talent.
galeriat20.com

CONJUNTO MONUMENTAL SAN JUAN DE DIOS
Murcia (Murcia)
A church featuring religious architecture, sculpture and paintings. It also houses the ancient ruins of Alcázar Mayor.
museosregiondemurcia.es

MUSEU DE SANTA CLARA
Murcia (Murcia)
This former palace has a storied history having housed Muslim emirs, Castilian monarchs and Poor Clare nuns. Don't miss the courtyard and the Arabic pool.
museosregiondemurcia.es

ANDALUCÍA

This large southern region – which is home to cities such as Seville and Granada, Tarifa and Málaga – is one of the country's most storied parts. In fact, Andalucía's history can be seen in everything from its Islamic-influenced architecture to the varied cuisine.

STAY

FINCA CORTESÍN
Casares
With four pools, sea views and its own golf course, Finca Cortesín is the perfect palm-studded escape.
fincacortesin.com

HOTEL BODEGA TÍO PEPE
Jerez de la Frontera
Luxury hotel in the heart of historic Jerez by the family behind the Tío Pepe winery
tiopepe.com

FINCA LA DONAIRA
Montecorto
A nine-room estate on a farm and equestrian centre in the Sierra de Grazalema mountains *(see page 26)*.
ladonaira.com

MARBELLA CLUB
Marbella
A beachside hotel that counts Audrey Hepburn and Grace Kelly among past guests. It offers excellent service, sprawling gardens and plenty of dining options *(see page 19)*.
marbellaclub.com

HOTEL ALFONSO XIII
Seville
Commissioned by the former King of Spain, this ornate hotel is a grand affair that fuses Andalucian, Moorish and Castilian styles *(see page 33)*.
theluxurycollection.com/seville

HOTEL MERCER SEVILLA
Seville
In Seville's historic centre by the Real Maestranza bullring, this grand hotel was a 19th century mansion and now features a rooftop terrace with pool and bar.
mercersevilla.com

A view of Vejer de la Frontera

HOTEL PALACIO DE VILLAPANÉS
Seville
A restored 18th-century palace with marble columns, a sunny terrace and parquet floors – as well as spacious rooms replete with mid-century furniture.
coolrooms.com/palaciovillapanes

PLÁCIDO Y GRATA
Seville
Another opulent offering, this bright 15-room hotel by architect Marta Santana features Scandinavian-inspired interiors with a neutral colour palette *(see page 32)*.
placidoygratahotel.com

BOUTIQUE HOTEL V
Vejer de la Frontera
The site dates back to the 16th century and offers a tranquil courtyard that's draped in greenery.
hotelv-vejer.com

PLAZA 18
Vejer de la Frontera
The Califa hospitality group rents 15 houses in the rural Andalician town, including the lavish, six-bedroom Plaza 18 *(see page 26)*.
califavejer.com/plaza-18

EAT & DRINK

EL FARO DE CÁDIZ
Cádiz
This third-generation family-run fish restaurant has been serving fine fare since 1946.
elfarodecadiz.com

TABERNA CASA MANTECA
Cádiz
With walls replete with bullfighting images, this taberna is known both for its authenticity and *chicharrónes* (fried pork rinds).
+34 956 213 603

EL CUARTEL DEL MAR
Chiclana de la Frontera
This chic beachside spot serves exceptional seafood – including regional bluefin tuna *(see page 49)*.
elcuarteldelmar.com

NOOR
Córdoba
Chef Paco Morales's two-Michelin-starred kitchen explores the region's cuisine when it was under Muslim rule *(see page 47)*.
noorrestaurant.es

BAR CANDELA
Granada
Informal tapas bar with a lively atmosphere and tasty dishes.
+34 958 227 010

LA COSMO
Málaga
A contemporary bistro with Andalucian influence (*see page 51*).
lacosmo.es

EL PIMPI
Málaga
This Málaga institution has been delighting diners since 1971 (*see page 50*).
elpimpi.com

EL RINCONCILLO
Seville
Sample a glass of regional wine with *carrillada* (pork-cheek stew) at Seville's oldest bar (*see page 72*).
elrinconcillo.es

CONTENEDOR
Seville
Contenedor is a low-key, bustling spot with an ever-changing menu.
restaurantecontenedor.com

LAS TERESAS
Seville
It doesn't get much more Seville than this authentic bar, which serves *cañas* and regional fare (*see page 48*).
lasteresas.es

SHOP

CASA LAMAR
Cádiz
Shop stocking an array of products all made in Cádiz.
casalamar.es

LA IMPORTADORA
Seville
Concept store selling art, fashion and homewares in Seville's centre.
laimportadora.es

ORANGERIE
Seville
Plant shop and florist supplying the city with locally-grown blooms (*see page 95*).
+34 663 328 429

POPULART
Seville
Characterful shop selling traditional handmade Spanish wares.
populartsevilla.com

TENDERETE SEVILLA
Seville
Stacks of colourful ceramics, textiles and basketry pad the shelves of this small but bright shop.
tenderete-sevilla.negocio.site

Playa La Caleta in Cádiz

DO

CENTRO DE CREACIÓN CONTEMPORÁNEA DE ANDALUCÍA
Córdoba
Known as the C3A centre, this artistic hub is a place for creative experimentation and development, it also showcases temporary exhibitions for the public.
c3a.es

ALHAMBRA
Granada
This palace and fortress is one of the best-preserved examples of Moorish architecture in Spain.
alhambra-patronato.es

MUSEO MEMORIA DE ANDALUCÍA
Granada
Museum showcasing the region's history and geography from Roman times through to the present day (*see page 154*).
cajagranadafundacion.es

TABANCO EL PASAJE
Jerez de la Frontera
A traditional taberna where authentic flamenco is performed daily (*see page 138*).
tabancoelpasaje.com

PICASSO MUSEUM
Málaga
Picasso's birth city has a museum devoted to his works, with some 200 pieces exhibited within.
museopicassomalaga.org

CAAC
Seville
The Centro Andaluz de Arte Contemporáneo boasts a collection scattered throughout the 14th-century monastery (*see page 132*).
caac.es

DELIMBO
Seville
Contemporary art gallery exhibiting everything from graffiti to graphic design (*see page 136*).
delimbo.com

FUNDACIÓN NMAC
Vejer de la Frontera
This open-air museum facilitates a dialogue between nature and art (*see page 130*).
fundacionnmac.org

CENTRE POMPIDOU MÁLAGA
Málaga
Looking like a Rubik's Cube from afar, this museum is an off-shoot of the original centre in France. It houses works by artists such as Francis Bacon and Frida Kahlo.
centrepompidou-malaga.eu

THE NORTH

The verdant north might not have the climate that the south boasts, but it more than makes up for it in its dramatic landscapes and dynamic cities – from Vigo and Santander to Bilbao and San Sebastián. Plus it has a world-renowned gastronomic offering, with a leading cultural scene to boot.

STAY

EL MÔDERNE HOTEL
Asturias (Gijón)
A restored art deco building is now home to the glitzy hotel in Gijón's centre (*see page 39*).
elmodernehotel.com

HOTEL TORRE DE VILLADEMOROS
Asturias (Villademoros)
An exclusive 11-room guesthouse with access to a private beach. Request the suite that's located in the site's medieval tower.
torrevillademoros.com

HOTEL LANDA
Burgos
This hotel and restaurant offers a glass-encased pool, medieval stone tower and four-poster beds.
landa.as

GRAN HOTEL DOMINE BILBAO
Bilbao
A sculptural hotel with views over the Guggenheim Bilbao designed by Spanish artists Javier Mariscal and Fernando Salas (*see page 35*).
hoteldominebilbao.com

GRAN HOTEL LA TOJA
Galicia (La Toja)
This glamorous resort is a favourite of the rich and famous – it even counts Spanish royalty among its past guests (*see page 21*).
eurostarshotels.com

CASA JOSEPHINE
La Rioja (Sorzano)
A five-bedroom guesthouse by Madrid-based designers Casa Josephine (*see page 27*).
casajosephine.com

HOTEL RESTAURANTE CASA GRANDE
La Rioja (Grañón)
This modern hotel is the perfect base to explore the region's wineries.
casagrandehotel.net

Fishing boats in Corrubedo, Galicia

AKELARRE
San Sebastián
A sleek spot by the owners of the three-Michelin-starred restaurant of the same name (*see page 20*).
akelarre.net

HOTEL ARBASO
San Sebastián
A well-appointed site in the city's Centro neighbourhood (*see page 34*).
hotelarbaso.com

HOTEL VILLA FAVORITA
San Sebastián
This grand hotel sits on the edge of La Concha beach.
hotelvillafavorita.com

MENDI ARGIA
San Sebastián
A small, design-focused hotel in the mountains above the city.
mendiargia.com

HACIENDA ZORITA WINE HOTEL & ORGANIC FARM
Salamanca
This former monastery dates from the 14th century (once frequented by Christopher Columbus) and now includes a winery and spa.
haciendazorita.com

EAT & DRINK

CASA MARCIAL
Asturias (Arriondas)
A world-class family-run restaurant serving local classics (*see page 57*).
casamarcial.es

EL CASINO BAR
Asturias (Cadavedo)
This former social club offers just one daily dish. Enjoy it on the sun-soaked patio.
+34 985 645 039

CASA CÁMARA
Basque Country (Pasai Donibane)
Diners at this seafood joint can hand-pick crustaceans from a trap that's lifted directly into the restaurant (*see page 55*).
casacamara.com

ASTARBE SAGARDOTEGIA
Basque Country (Astigarraga)
Basque cider is made in the traditional way at this family-run establishment (*see page 79*).
astarbe.eus

BASCOOK
Bilbao
Chef and owner Aitor Elizegi is known for serving regional dishes with a Japanese twist (*see page 56*).
bascook.com

BOCADERO BILBAO
Bilbao
The earthy-toned interior plays host to a Mediterranean-inspired menu.
bocaderobilbao.com

ERRIBERA MERKATUA
Bilbao
The largest covered market in Europe with an excellent street-food hall (see page 83).
Erribera Kalea

GURE TOKI
Bilbao
This restaurant offers a contemporary take on Basque cuisine (see page 56).
guretoki.com

LA MOZZERIA DE BIRIBIL
Bilbao
Cheese factory owned by three friends who make exceptional Italian-style dairy products.
biribilbrothers.com

LA OKA
Bilbao
Premium food shop selling top-quality meat and charcuterie from regional farms.
laoka.es

RÍO OJA
Bilbao
An authentic no-frills spot serving traditional Basque casseroles.
+34 944 150 871

VÍCTOR MONTES
Bilbao
This Bilbao establishment has been running since 1846 and is the location where the Guggenheim museum deal was signed.
victormontes.com

COBO ESTRATOS
Burgos
A Michelin-starred site that offers a refined take on regional classics.
coboestratos.com

LA FAVORITA BURGOS
Burgos
This cosy taberna is well known for its quality *pintxos* and extensive wine list.
lafavoritaburgos.com

RESTAURANTE EL BODEGÓN
Cantabria (San Vicente de la Barquera)
A 40-minute drive from Santander, this fish restaurant serves an excellent set lunch menu.
elbodegonsvb.com

Cattle farmer Michel Rios

BAR DO PORTO
Galicia (Corrubedo)
David Chipperfield's place is perfect for a hearty meal (the octopus is a highlight) and a drink with the locals (see page 59).
+34 981 865 370

CAFÉ BAR EL MUELLE
Galicia (Santiago de Compostela)
This storied café was frequented by writers and intellectuals in the 1930s (see page 67).
elmuelle1931.com/pages/cafe-bar

CERVECERÍA ESTRELLA GALICIA
Galicia (A Coruña)
Estrella Galicia's crisp golden lager is best enjoyed in the brewery's northern hometown (see page 78).
estrellagalicia.es

GÓMEZ CRUZADO
La Rioja (Haro)
A family-run vineyard in Spain's famed wine region (see page 70).
gomezcruzado.com

CAFÉ IRUÑA
Pamplona
This grand café has remained largely unchanged since the days when it was visited by Ernest Hemingway (see page 67).
cafeiruna.com

CASA UROLA
San Sebastián
Chef Pablo Loureiro Rodil cut his teeth at his family's restaurant before launching Casa Urola.
casaurolajatetxea.es

GANBARA
San Sebastián
Opened in 1984, Ganbara was one of the first *pintxo* spots to open in the city (see page 54).
ganbarajatetxea.com

GANDARIAS
San Sebastián
This restaurant in the city's Old Town offers *pintxos* alfresco with refined fare served inside.
restaurantegandarias.com

MATALAUVA
San Sebastián
A cosy spot in the city's Gros neighbourhood has an inventive menu: each dish is comprised of no more than three ingredients.
matalauvagros.es

OHBABA
San Sebastián
The first plant-based coffee shop in northern Spain (*see page 69*).
ohbabakofi.com

OLD TOWN COFFEE
San Sebastián
An industrial-look speciality coffee shop run by three friends.
oldtowncoffeeroasters.com

REKONDO
San Sebastián
Rekondo restaurant has a collection of more than 100,000 bottles in its expansive cellar (*see page 54*).
rekondo.com

THE LOAF
San Sebastián
Popular sourdough bakery and speciality coffee spot (*see page 62*).
theloaf.eus

LA CASETA DE BOMBAS
Santander
This welcoming restaurant serves upmarket fare in the city's spacious former pump room (*see page 58*).
lacasetadebombas.es

MERCADO DE LA ESPERANZA
Santander
The Market of Hope, as it translates, is the place to buy exceptional seafood (*see page 82*).
Plaza de la Esperanza

EL MOLINO
Vigo
Upmarket *pastelería* that sells treats such as chocolate truffles, cakes and *coquitos*, Spanish coconut biscuits.
elmolinovigo.com

SHOP

TREKU
Basque Country (Zarautz)
This furniture brand is known for its playful designs (*see page 188*).
treku.com

ALONSO
Bilbao
Old-school men's shoe shop that opened in 1940 (*see page 109*).
calzadosalonso.com

Pimientos de Padrón

LIBRERÍA ANTICUARIA ASTARLOA
Bilbao
A bookshop that has been buying and selling rare titles since the 1990s.
libreriastarloa.com

PERSUADE
Bilbao
This concept store is a treasure trove offering a curated collection of clothing, fragrances and antiques (*see page 100*).
persuade.es

MAN 1924
Bilbao
A cult classic favoured by Spain's best dressed for its laidback menswear (*see page 106*).
man1924.com

D-DUE
Galicia (Rianxo)
Womenswear brand that makes characteristic linen designs with loose silhouettes (*see page 105*).
d-due.com

MASSCOB
Galicia (A Coruña)
Expect relaxed dresses, trousers and jackets from Masscob's coveted collection (*see page 104*).
masscob.com

SARGADELOS
Galicia (Cervo)
Ceramics company known for its distinctive blue-and-white crockery (*see page 93*).
sargadelos.com

MANTAS EZCARAY
La Rioja (Ezcaray)
Third-generation family-run textiles brand that crafts sumptuously soft scarves and blankets (*see page 88*).
mantasezcaray.com

ALMACENES ARENZANA
San Sebastián
Selling raw materials and finished goods, this craft and textiles shop opened in 1900 and is still run by the same family.
almacenesarenzana.com

CASA PONSOL
San Sebastián
The original hat shop was founded by milliner Bernardo Ponsol in 1838 and is the best-known spot to find a Basque beret (*see page 99*).
casaponsol.com

LIBRERÍA DONOSTI
San Sebastián
Librería Donosti stocks everything from children's books to literary fiction (*see page 141*).
+34 943 424 688

LOREAK MENDIAN
San Sebastián
Clothing brand known for its comfy tees and knitwear (*see page 104*).
loreakmendian.com

DO

OSCAR NIEMEYER INTERNATIONAL CULTURAL CENTRE
Asturias (Avilés)
Stark white and sculptural, this art centre is the work of Oscar Niemeyer and it hosts theatrical performances, exhibitions and more.
centroniemeyer.es

UNIVERSIDAD LABORAL DE GIJÓN
Asturias (Gijón)
This vast cultural centre was originally conceived as an orphanage. There are also gardens, a restaurant and tower with spectacular views of Gijón (*see page 135*).
laboralciudaddelacultura.com

GALERÍA ESPACIO MARZANA
Bilbao
Gallery along the Río Nervión that exhibits new and established artists.
espaciomarzana.com

GUGGENHEIM MUSEUM BILBAO
Bilbao
New York City's contemporary art institution opened a Bilbao outpost in 1997, its shining structure designed by Canadian-American architect Frank Gehry (*see page 127*).
guggenheim-bilbao.eus

CHILLIDA LEKU
Basque Country (Hernani)
Sculpture park dedicated to Eduardo Chillida. Visitors can wander the farmhouse once owned by the artist and his wife (*see page 124*).
museochillidaleku.com

Galicia's Ria de Arousa

MUSEO DE LA EVOLUCIÓN HUMANA
Burgos
On the banks of the Río Arlanzón, this expansive building houses one of the most impressive collections of human fossils and archeological finds in the world.
museoevolucionhumana.com

EL CAPRICHO DE GAUDÍ
Cantabria (Comillas)
One of Gaudí's lesser-known creations, this house is one of the artist's few projects outside his native Cataluña.
elcaprichodegaudi.com

MUSEO SAN TELMO
San Sebastián
Former convent that exhibits objects and information about Basque history and culture.
santelmomuseoa.eus

VILLA MAGDALENA
San Sebastián
Founded by local curator Cy Schnabel, this gallery combines an international eye with local talent.
villamagdalena33.com

CENTRO BOTÍN
Santander
This cultural centre is an icon set beside Santander Bay (*see page 135*).
centrobotin.org

CLUB MARÍTIMO DE CANIDO
Vigo
Yacht club offering not only sailing lessons but a clubhouse with mid-century branding and plenty of well-to-do members (*see page 191*).
cmcanido.es

BALEARIC ISLANDS

This sunny set of isles on the Mediterranean – comprising Ibiza, Mallorca, Menorca and Formentera – has long been on the holiday hit list. Here, we introduce the best hotels, restaurants, shops and cultural spots to add to your itinerary.

STAY

NOBU HOTEL IBIZA BAY
Ibiza (Ibiza town)
From the team behind the culinary icon, this resort offers top fare in an unbeatable setting only 10 minutes from the city's buzz.
nobuhotelibizabay.com

SIX SENSES IBIZA
Ibiza (San Juan Bautista)
A masterclass in luxury, this hotel from the Six Senses group offers everything you'd expect and more (*see page 16*).
sixsenses.com

CAP ROCAT
Mallorca (Cala Blava)
A former fortress, this elegant hotel has breathtaking sea views. Book a room with a private pool chiselled into the rockface (*see page 15*).
caprocat.com

CAN BORDOY
Mallorca (Palma)
A Mallorquín palace has been turned into Palma's most talked-about hotel (*see page 36*).
canbordoy.com

ES RACÓ D'ARTÀ
Mallorca (Cami des Racó)
This converted 13th-century farmhouse is surrounded by vineyards, almond and olive trees. It offers the perfect rural escape with excellent fare (*see page 23*).
esracodarta.com

CRISTINE BEDFOR
Menorca (Mahón)
Guesthouse only moments from the city's shops and restaurants with a verdant garden and lap pool.
cristinebedforhotel.com

MENORCA EXPERIMENTAL
Menorca (Camí de Llucalari)
Bright interiors are paired with a hidden cliffside locale and inventive food and drink offering (*see page 22*).
menorcaexperimental.com

El Silencio Ibiza

TORRALBENC
Menorca (Cala'n Porter)
A converted Menorquín farmhouse, complete with a winery and award-winning restaurant.
torralbenc.com

EAT & DRINK

CASA JONDAL
Ibiza (Cala Jondal)
This chic beach restaurant and coveted lunch spot is headed by ex-El Bulli chef Rafael Zafra.
casajondal.es

ES XARCU
Ibiza (Porroig)
A family-run restaurant with a reputation for serving some of the island's best seafood (*see page 60*).
esxarcurestaurante.com

MAISON LE VRAI
Ibiza (Ibiza town)
Head to this restaurant for its innovative French fare and lively atmosphere.
maisonlevrai.com

SES ESCOLES
Ibiza (Sant Joan de Labritja)
A refined spot known for its traditional Ibizan dishes and exceptional olive oil, which is available to buy at the onsite shop.
sesescoles.com

CA NA TONETA
Mallorca (Caimari)
Sister-run restaurant that offers refined six-course tasting menus.
canatoneta.com

ARUME
Mallorca (Palma)
Sleek sushi bar in Santa Catalina. Owner Tomeu Martí also runs a fine-dining restaurant and sake bar (the island's first).
tomeumarti.com

CAV
Mallorca (Palma)
Wine bar and shop that sells a selection of tipples.
cavvins.com

EL BUNGALOW
Mallorca (Palma)
This old-school fish restaurant overlooks the Playa Ciudad Jardín.
+34 971 262 738

FORN DE LA GLÒRIA
Mallorca (Palma)
Palma's oldest bakery known for its excellent *ensaimadas*.
+34 971 713 317

ROSA DEL MAR RESTAURANTE
Mallorca (Palma)
An upmarket port-side restaurant complete with a nightclub.
rosadelmarrestaurante.com

EL CAMINO
Mallorca (Carrer de Can Brondo)
Exceptional tapas served at an elegant bar (*see page 61*).
elcaminopalma.es

HELADERÍA CA'N MIQUEL
Mallorca (Carrer dels Montcades)
This ice-cream institution offers innovative flavours (*see page 65*).
heladeriacanmiquel.com

LA MOLIENDA
Mallorca (Palma)
The island's first speciality coffee shop (*see page 69*).
lamolienda.es

BINIFADET
Menorca (Sant Lluís)
Winery and restaurant – opt for the tasting menu with wine pairing to sample each of the vineyard's tipples.
binifadet.com

CAP ROIG
Menorca (Cala Sa Mesquida)
Founded in 1983, this seafood joint is a local institution that sits on the cliffs above Cala Sa Mesquida.
restaurantcaproig.com

NONNA BAZAAR
Menorca (Ciutadella)
This rural farmhouse is now a chic courtyard restaurant, which serves dishes made with local and homegrown produce. It's an idyllic spot to enjoy cocktails at sunset.
nonnabazaar.com

RESTAURANTE MIRAMAR
Menorca (Calas Fonts)
This traditional tapas spot in the picturesque Calas Fonts serves some of the best tapas on the island.
+34 971 364 643

MERCAT DES PEIX
Menorca (Mahón)
Visit early in the morning for the day's catch or in the evening when it transforms into a tapas bar.
Plaza de España

ULISSES
Menorca (Ciutadella)
Seafood restaurant with a focus on Balearic fare with a menu that changes daily (*see page 61*).
ulissesbar.com

The best way to get around Ibiza

SHOP

CORTANA
Mallorca (Palma)
Rosa Esteva's flagship store, which sells the fashion designer's limited-edition womenswear. Think soft linen dresses, cashmere wraps and elegant accessories.
cortana.es

LA PRINCIPAL
Mallorca (Palma)
Clothing shop stocking brands including Sebago and Costume National, as well as leather products from the La Principal owners' label Mews.
laprincipalshop.com

ARQUINESIA
Mallorca (Palma)
Perfumerie in Palma's Old Town known for its natural scents and candles (*see page 94*).
arquinesia.com

LA CERERIA
Menorca (Mahón)
This small multibrand shop in Menorca's capital is filled with luxury womenswear curated by the ever-stylish owner.
lacereriamenorca.com

KINIRIA
Menorca (Ciutadella)
Timeless leather handbags and accessories handmade on the island (*see page 94*).
kiniria.com

DO

PALMA SPORT & TENNIS CLUB
Mallorca (Palma)
This modern social club boasts five clay courts, a swimming pool and gym for sporty sorts with a bistro and spa to unwind in (*see page 191*).
palmatennis.com

PELAIRES
Mallorca (Palma)
Opened in 1969, Pelaires is Spain's longest-running contemporary art gallery (*see page 136*).
pelaires.com

ENCANT
Menorca (Mahón)
Mahón's Encant commercial gallery exhibits contemporary artwork behind its teal-hued shutters.
encant.net

HAUSER & WIRTH MENORCA
Menorca (Mahón)
This gallery boasts a landscaped garden and sculpture trail, as well as a shop and sun-dappled restaurant (*see page 128*).
menorca.hauserwirth.com

CANARY ISLANDS

The Canary Islands are too often dismissed for their package-holiday history. In reality, this archipelago has plenty to discover – from inky-hued beaches and volcanic scenery to luxury hotels and compelling cultural sites. It's time to set sail for this oft-forgotten corner of Spain.

STAY

HOTEL PALACIO ICO
Lanzarote (Teguise)
This whitewashed guesthouse dates from the 1690s and boasts a palm-tree-lined courtyard, coffered ceilings and spacious rooms with four-poster beds (see page 35).
hotelpalacioico.com

HACIENDA CUATRO VENTANAS
Tenerife (Los Realejos)
A sprawling estate with six luxury villas. The hotel offers tropical gardens (with more than 100 palm trees) and a pool with striking coastal views (see page 21).
haciendacuatroventanas.com

HOTEL LA QUINTA ROJA
Tenerife (Garachico)
A characterful baroque-style mansion with ancient stone walls and an original wooden structure that opens into a tranquil courtyard.
quintaroja.com

LA LAGUNA GRAN HOTEL
Tenerife (La Laguna)
This emblematic hotel combines modern design with its historical setting at the heart of the town of La Laguna, a Unesco World Heritage Site.
lalagunagranhotel.com

EAT & DRINK

RESTAURANTE DUNAS DE FAMARA
Lanzarote (Teguise)
This spectacular restaurant sits in the shadows of the Riscos de Famara cliffs while overlooking the beach. Punters can settle down with a cocktail at sunset or enjoy the seasonal menu of Canary classics.
restaurantedunasdefamara.com

Charco de la Laja in Tenerife

BODEGAS VIÑÁTIGO
Tenerife (El Convento)
Fifth-generation family-run winery that has cultivated 13 of Tenerife's native grapes (see page 71).
bodegasvinatigo.com

MIRADOR DE GARACHICO
Tenerife (Garachico)
This hilltop restaurant serves traditional Canary cuisine with a modern twist – and with stunning coastal views to boot.
+34 922 831 198

TASCA 61
Tenerife (La Laguna)
This pint-sized restaurant has a delicious menu of daily specials, including regional cheeses and beer from a Tenerife eco-brewery.
tasca61.com

DO

CASA DE COLÓN
Gran Canaria (Las Palmas)
The former home of Christopher Columbus exhibits the explorer's belongings, including drawings, journals and furniture.
casadecolon.com

AUDITORIO DE TENERIFE
Tenerife (La Laguna)
Located near the port of Santa Cruz, the auditorium houses the island's Symphony Orchestra (see page 139).
auditoriodetenerife.com

TENERIFE ESPACIO DE LAS ARTES
Tenerife (La Laguna)
Known as TEA, the art centre was designed by Herzog & de Meuron and always has something to offer: exhibitions, films and workshops.
teatenerife.es

JAMEOS DEL AGUA
Lanzarote (Punta Mujeres)
The cultural complex includes restaurants, bars, an auditorium and a swimming pool built into and around a volcanic cave with a subterranean lake (see page 152).
cactlanzarote.com

JARDÍN DEL CACTUS
Lanzarote (Guatiza)
One of the world's largest cactus gardens that houses some 4,500 cacti of around 500 differing species – from five continents.
cactlanzarote.com

SPAIN
The MONOCLE Handbook

INDEX

51 del Sol (El), *Aranda del Duero* 199

A

A Coruña 78, 104, 210
Abadía Retuerta LeDomaine, *Valladolid* 25, 199
Ábbatte, *Segovia* 89, 117, 199
Absoluta Flora, *Valencia* 205
Acueducto de Segovia, *Segovia* 199
Akelarre, *San Sebastián* 20, 209
Al Júcar 116
Albarrán Bourdais, *Madrid* 193, 198
Alemanys 5, *Girona* 203
Alhambra, *Granada* 208
Alicante 39, 111, 113, 126, 145, 206
Alma Nomad, *Madrid* 63, 197
Almacenes Arenzana, *San Sebastián* 211
Alonso, *Bilbao* 109, 211
Alzueta, *Barcelona* 137, 202
Andalucía 8, 19, 26, 47, 49, 50, 51, 130, 138, 148, 154, 162, 167, 174—175, 176—177, 207—208
Antigua Casa de Guardia, *Málaga* 176
Après Ski, *Barcelona* 201
Aranda del Duero 199
Arquinesia, *Mallorca* 94, 214
Arriondas 57, 209
Arroz Catalá Valencia 119
Artesanía Gonzalez 117
Arume, *Mallorca* 213
Astarbe Sagardotegia, *Astigarraga* 79, 209
Astigarraga 79, 209
Asturias 39, 57, 97, 135, 160, 209, 212
Atrio, *Cáceres* 37, 199
Auditorio de Tenerife, *Tenerife* 139, 215
Avilés 212

B

Baldomero, *Barcelona* 42, 200
Balea 121
Balearic Islands 8, 15, 16, 22, 23, 36, 38, 60, 61, 69, 94, 128—129, 136, 167, 184, 182—183, 186, 187, 191, 192, 213—214
Balius, *Madrid* 76, 201

Banyoles 110, 118, 203
Bar Brutal, *Barcelona* 200
Bar Candela, *Granada* 207
Bar Central, *Barcelona* 76
Bar Cock, *Madrid* 75, 196
Bar Cugat, *Barcelona* 200
Bar do Porto, *Corrubedo* 59, 210
Bar El Frances, *Tarifa* 175
Bàrbara Forés, *Tarragona* 70, 120, 203
Barcelona
 STAY 30, 31, 200
 EAT & DRINK 41, 42, 43, 44, 62, 68, 76, 200—201
 SHOP 87, 90—91, 103, 110, 189, 201—202
 DO 112, 125, 127, 130, 137, 138, 143, 145, 141, 146, 150—151, 185, 202
Bardero, *Madrid* 196
Bascook, *Bilbao* 56, 209
Basque Country 10—11, 20, 25, 34, 35, 54, 55, 56, 62, 69, 79, 83, 99, 100, 104, 106, 109, 124, 127, 141, 155, 165, 188, 209—212
Bassal, *Barcelona* 103, 202
Begur 18, 203
Bernardo Estévez Chánselus 121
Bilbao 35, 56, 83, 100, 106, 109, 127, 209—212
Binifadet, *Menorca* 128—129, 214
Bionda (La), *Begur* 18, 203
Bluebell Coffee Roasters, *Valencia* 171, 205
Boca de Vin, *Alicante* 206
Bocadero Bilbao, *Bilbao* 210
Bodegas Habla 119
Bodegas Rosell, *Madrid* 196
Bodegas Viñátigo, *Tenerife* 71, 215
Bombas Gens, *Valencia* 205
Boutique Hotel V, *Vejer de la Frontera* 207
Brote (El), *Madrid* 197
Brutus de Gaper, *Barcelona* 201
Bungalow (El), *Mallorca* 213
Burgos 185, 209—212

C

Ca na Toneta, *Mallorca* 213
CAAC, *Seville* 132—133, 208
Cáceres 37, 131, 199
Cadaqués 17, 203
Cádiz 207—208

Café Bar el Muelle, *Santiago de Compostela* 67, 210
Café Iruña, *Pamplona* 67, 210
Café le Bistrot, *Girona* 203
Cafés Pozo 116
Cala Macarelleta, *Menorca* 167
Calpe 145
Camino (El), *Mallorca* 61, 214
Camping, *Barcelona* 201
Can Bordoy, *Mallorca* 36, 213
Canalla Bistro, *Valencia* 171
Candela en Rama, *Valencia* 99, 205
Canoa Lab, *Valencia* 92, 114, 205
Cantabria 58, 135, 160, 210, 212
Cap Rocat, *Mallorca* 15, 38, 213
Cap Roig, *Menorca* 214
Capas Seseña, *Madrid* 107, 198
Capricho de Gaudí (El), *Comillas* 212
Capullo 121
Carpintería (La), *Vigo* 172
Casa Bonay, *Barcelona* 31, 200
Casa Boumort, *Lleida* 203
Casa Cámara, *Pasai Donibane* 55, 209
Casa Carmela, *Valencia* 204
Casa de Colón, *Gran Canaria* 215
Casa de Diego, *Madrid* 97, 115, 198
Casa Encendida (La), *Madrid* 134, 198
Casa Fidel, *Madrid* 197
Casa González & González, *Madrid* 113, 197
Casa Jondal, *Ibiza* 213
Casa Josephine, *Sorzano* 27, 186, 209
Casa Lamar, *Cádiz* 208
Casa Marcial, *Arriondas* 57, 209
Casa Mariol 119
Casa Mira 119
Casa Museo Salvador Dalí, *Portlligat* 123, 203
Casa Nereta, *Cadaqués* 17, 203
Casa Ponsol, *San Sebastián* 99, 211
Casa Urola, *San Sebastián* 211
Casa Vicens, *Barcelona* 146, 202
Caseta de Bombas (La), *Santander* 58, 211
Casino Bar (El), *Arriondas* 209
Castañer, *Banyoles* 110, 118, 203
Castilla y Léon 24, 25, 38, 89, 160, 185, 199
Cav, *Mallorca* 213
CCCC, *Valencia* 205
Centre de Cultura Contemporània de Barcelona, *Barcelona* 202

INDEX

Centre Pompidou, *Málaga* 208
Centro Botín, *Santander* 135, 212
Centro de Creación Contemporánea de Andalucía, *Córdoba* 208
Cerámica los Arrayanes 116
Cereria (La), *Menorca* 214
Cervexería Nós, *Vigo* 172
Cervo 93, 211
Chandal, *Barcelona* 201
Chiclana de la Frontera 49, 207
Chico (El), *Madrid* 198
Chillida Leku, *Hernani* 124, 212
Chiringuito el Ocho, *Valencia* 204
Chuchis Bar (Los), *Madrid* 197
Ciudad de las Artes y las Ciencias, *Valencia* 147, 205
Cloudstreet Bakery, *Barcelona* 62, 200
Club Marítimo de Canido, *Vigo* 191, 212
Club Matador, *Madrid* 190
Cobo Estratos, *Burgos* 185, 210
Cocol, *Madrid* 98, 115, 117, 118, 120, 197
ColaCao 114
Colmada (La), *Madrid* 197
Comillas 212
Compartir, *Cadaqués* 203
Conjunto Monumental San Juan de Dios, *Murcia* 206
Contain, *Mallorca* 186
Contenedor, *Seville* 208
Córdoba 47, 143, 148, 207—208
Corrubedo 59, 209, 210
Cortana, *Mallorca* 214
Cosmo (La), *Málaga* 51, 208
Cosmopolita Malagueña (La), *Málaga* 176
Costa Brava 17, 18, 137, 203
Cotton House, *Barcelona* 30, 200
Coush Armó, *Barcelona* 201
Cristine Bedfor, *Menorca* 213
Crunat, *Alicante* 113
Cuartel del Mar (El), *Chiclana de la Frontera* 49, 207
Cubiña, *Barcelona* 189, 201
Cuenca 199
Cuit Espai Ceràmic, *Valencia* 171

D

D-Due, *Rianxo* 105, 211
Dama (La), *Barcelona* 200
Dani Brasserie, *Madrid* 73, 197
Delimbo, *Seville* 136, 208
Deluz y Compañía 58, 85
Duquesita (La), *Madrid* 64, 196

E

Ecoalf, *Madrid* 109, 197
Edit 32, *Valencia* 205
Eines (Les), *Barcelona* 201
Emilio Arias Lizano 114
Encant, *Menorca* 214
Eroica Caffè, *Barcelona* 200
Erribera Merkatua, *Bilbao* 83, 210
Es Racó d'Artà, *Mallorca* 23, 213
Es Xarcu, *Ibiza* 60, 213
Espacio Valverde, *Madrid* 137, 198
Espai Xavier Corberó, *Barcelona* 150—151
Estrella Galicia, *A Coruña* 78, 93, 116, 210
Eurostars Pórtico Alicante, *Alicante* 206
Extremadura 37, 113, 131, 199
Ezcaray 88, 211

F

Fábrica (La), *Madrid* 197
Fábrica de Hielo (La), *Valencia* 204
Faro de Cádiz (El), *Cádiz* 207
Favorita Burgos (La), *Burgos* 210
Federal, *Valencia* 204
Finca Cortesín, *Casares* 207
Finca la Donaira, *Montecorto* 26, 207
Fiskebar, *Barcelona* 200
Fismuler, *Madrid* 196
Flor de Calasparra 120
Fonda Pepa, *Barcelona* 43, 201
Formaje, *Madrid* 84, 196
Formentera 164, 182—183
Forn de la Glòria, *Mallorca* 213
Four Seasons Hotel Madrid, *Madrid* 73, 196, 197
Fran Café, *Valencia* 193, 205
Freses (Les), *Jesús Pobre* 206
Fuente Aceña Hotel Boutique, *Duero Valley* 199

Fundació Joan Miró, *Barcelona* 125, 202
Fundación Antonio Pérez, *Cuenca* 199
Fundación María Cristina Masaveu Peterson, *Madrid* 198
Fundación NMAC, *Vejer de la Frontera* 130, 208
Funky Bakers Eatery, *Barcelona* 200

G

Galería Espacio Marzana, *Bilbao* 212
Galería Rosa Santos, *Valencia* 205
Galería T20, *Murcia* 143, 206
Galería Vangar, *Valencia* 205
Galicia 21, 59, 67, 78, 93, 103, 104, 105, 153, 163, 172—173, 180—181, 191, 209—212
Ganbara, *San Sebastián* 54, 210
Gandarias, *San Sebastián* 210
Garcia Madrid, *Madrid* 198
Garcima 119
GCA Architects, *Barcelona* 185
Gijón 39, 135, 209, 212
Girona 44, 203
Glent, *Madrid* 111, 198
Gómez Cruzado, *Haro* 70, 121, 210
Gota, *Madrid* 74, 197
Gran Café Santander, *Madrid* 66, 197
Gran Canaria 215
Gran Hotel Domine Bilbao, *Bilbao* 35, 209
Gran Hotel Inglés, *Madrid* 29, 196
Gran Hotel La Toja, *La Toja* 21, 209
Gran Martínez, *Valencia* 77, 204
Gran Rhin Bar, *Murcia* 206
Granada 154, 207—208
Granja Vendrell, *Barcelona* 44, 200
Gresca, *Barcelona* 41, 200
Guggenheim Museum Bilbao, *Bilbao* 127, 210
Gure Toki, *Bilbao* 56, 210

H

Hacienda Cuatro Ventanas, *Tenerife* 21, 215
Hacienda Zorita Wine Hotel & Organic Farm, *Salamanca* 209
Haro 70, 210

Hauser & Wirth Menorca,
 Menorca 128—129, 214
Hayon Studio 112
Heladería Ca'n Miquel, *Mallorca* 65, 214
Helga de Alvear, *Cáceres* 131, 199
Hereu, *Barcelona* 110, 117, 202
Hernani 124
Heyshop, *Barcelona* 202
Horno Santo Cristo 118
Hospes Amérigo, *Alicante* 206
Hotel Alfonso XIII, *Seville* 33, 207
Hotel Arbaso, *San Sebastián* 34, 209
Hotel Bodega Tío Pepe, *Jerez de la Frontera* 207
Hotel Brummell, *Barcelona* 200
Hotel la Quinta Roja, *Tenerife* 215
Hotel Landa, *Burgos* 209
Hotel Mercer Sevilla, *Seville* 207
Hotel Palacio de Villapanés, *Seville* 207
Hotel Palacio Ico, *Lanzarote* 35, 215
Hotel Pulitzer, *Barcelona* 200
Hotel Restaurant Casa Grande, *Grañón* 209
Hotel Serawa, *Alicante* 39, 206
Hotel Torre de Villademoros, *Villademoros* 209
Hotel Villa Favorita, *San Sebastián* 209
Huguet, *Mallorca* 187

I

Ibiza 16, 60, 213—214
IKB191, *Madrid* 189, 197
Ikigai Velázquez, *Madrid* 197
Importadora (La), *Seville* 208
Islas Cies, *Galicia* 163, 173
Ivam, *Valencia* 205
Jameos del Agua, *Lanzarote* 152, 215
Jardí del Turia, *Valencia* 205
Jardín del Cactus, *Lanzarote* 215
Jardines del Palacio Real de la Granja, *Real Sitio de San Ildefonso* 199

J

Jávea 25, 206
Javier S Medina Carpinteria 28, *Madrid* 96, 198
Jerez Arquitectos, *Burgos* 185
Jerez de la Frontera 138, 207—208
Jesús Pobre 206
Joncake, *Barcelona* 200
Josefita, *Madrid* 53, 197

K

Kiniria, *Menorca* 94, 214

L

La Rioja 27, 70, 88, 186, 209—212
Lacuesta 116
Laguna Gran Hotel (La), *Tenerife* 215
Lanzarote 35, 152, 157, 215
Lhardy, *Madrid* 52, 197
Librería Anticuaria Astarloa, *Bilbao* 211
Librería Donosti, *San Sebastián* 141, 212
Librería Terranova, *Barcelona* 141, 202
Llibreria Finestres, *Barcelona* 201
Llop Madrid, *Madrid* 101, 198
Loaf (The), *San Sebastián* 62, 211
Loewe, *Madrid* 96, 107, 117, 118, 198
Loreak Mendian, *San Sebastián* 104, 212
Luis Adelantado, *Valencia* 205
Lukan Gourmet 121

M

MACA, *Alicante* 126, 206
MACBA, *Barcelona* 202
Madrid
  STAY 28, 29, 196
  EAT & DRINK 52, 53, 63, 64, 66, 68, 73, 74, 75, 80, 84, 196—197
  SHOP 96, 97, 98, 101, 102, 103, 107, 108, 109, 111, 113, 189, 197—198
  DO 131, 134, 137, 140, 149, 178—179, 186, 190, 193, 198

Madrid Edition (The), *Madrid* 29, 196
Maestro Sierra (El) 120
Magro Cardona, *Madrid* 198
Mahou 116
Maison Le Vrai, *Ibiza* 213
Málaga 50, 51, 127, 143, 176—177, 208
Mallorca 15, 23, 36, 61, 65, 69, 94, 136, 161, 184, 186, 187, 191, 192, 213—214
Man 1924, *Bilbao* 106, 211
Mandarin Oriental Ritz, *Madrid* 196
Mantas Ezcaray, *Ezcaray* 88, 211
Marbella 19, 207
Marbella Club, *Marbella* 19, 207
Margarita, *Costa Brava* 203
Marset 116
Marugal 38
Masscob, *A Coruña* 104, 211
Matalauva, *San Sebastián* 210
Mendi Argia, *San Sebastián* 209
Menorca 22, 61, 94, 128—129, 167, 213—214
Menorca Experimental, *Menorca* 22, 213
Mercabanyal, *Valencia* 204
Mercado Central de Atarazanas, *Málaga* 176
Mercado Central de Valencia, *Valencia* 81, 85, 204
Mercado de Correos, *Murcia* 206
Mercado de la Esperanza, *Santander* 82, 211
Mercado de Vallehermoso, *Madrid* 80, 196
Mercat des Peix, *Menorca* 214
Mercato Ballaró, *Madrid* 196
Mercer Hotel Barcelona, *Barcelona* 200
Mezquita-Catedral de Córdoba, *Córdoba* 148
Microteatro Por Dinero, *Madrid* 198
Mirador de Garachico, *Tenerife* 215
Misia, *Madrid* 197
MNAC, *Barcelona* 202
Môderne Hotel (El), *Gijón* 39, 209
Molienda (La), *Mallorca* 69, 214
Molino (El), *Vigo* 211
Mòlt Bakery, *Valencia* 204
Montecorto 26, 207
Mozzeria de Biribil (La), *Bilbao* 210
Muralla Roja (La), *Calpe* 145
Murcia 47, 143, 206

INDEX

Museo de Arte Abstracto Español, *Cuenca* 199
Museo de Arte Contemporáneo Helga de Alvear, *Cáceres* 199
Museo de la Evolución Humana, *Burgos* 212
Museo Memoria de Andalucía, *Granada* 154, 208
Museo Reina Sofía, *Madrid* 131, 198
Museo San Telmo, *San Sebastián* 212
Museo Sorolla, *Madrid* 198
Museu Can Framis, *Barcelona* 130, 202
Museu de Santa Clara, *Murcia* 206
Museu del Disseny, *Barcelona* 202
Museu Picasso, *Barcelona* 127, 202

N

Nanimarquina, *Barcelona* 87, 189, 201
Natif, *Madrid* 196
Nau (La), *Barcelona* 202
Navarre 11, 67
Nobu Hotel Ibiza Bay, *Ibiza* 213
Nomad Coffee, *Barcelona* 32, 68, 201
Nomad Hotel Xàbia Port, *Jávea* 206
Nonna Bazaar, *Menorca* 214
Noor, *Córdoba* 47, 207
Normal, *Girona* 44, 203
Nozomi, *Valencia* 205
Número C, *Tarifa* 175
Nuñez de Prado 114

O

Obrador de Antequera 119
Ohbaba, *San Sebastián* 69, 211
Ohlab 36, 184
Oka (La), *Bilbao* 210
Olavide Bar de Libros, *Madrid* 197
Old Town Coffee, *San Sebastián* 211
Olives, *Galicia* 180–181
Oller del Mas, *Manresa* 203
Only You Hotel, *Valencia* 204
Orangerie, *Seville* 95, 208
Ortiz 114
Orval, *Barcelona* 201
Oscar Niemeyer International Cultural Centre, *Avilés* 212
Ostras Pedrín, *Valencia* 46, 205
Oteyza, *Madrid* 108, 197

P

Palacio Vallier, *Valencia* 204
Palanca Carnissers, *Valencia* 85, 204
Palau de la Música Catalana, *Barcelona* 138, 189, 202
Pallares Solsona 115
Palma Sport & Tennis Club, *Mallorca* 191, 214
Palmaria 114
Pamplona 67, 210
Paperground, *Madrid* 140, 198
Parador d'Aiguablava, *Costa Brava* 203
Parador de Cuenca, *Cuenca* 199
Parador de Segovia, *Segovia* 24, 199
Parking Pizza, *Barcelona* 200
Parque Rural de Anaga, *Tenerife* 158–159
Parra (La), *Madrid* 53, 196
Pasai Donibane 55, 209
Pedro García, *Madrid* 111, 198
Pelaires, *Mallorca* 136, 214
Peña Tierra Aranda, *Aranda del Duero* 199
Peninsula de Llevant, *Mallorca* 161
Pepica (La), *Valencia* 45, 204
Perelló 120
Persuade, *Bilbao* 100, 211
Pez, *Madrid* 102, 197
Phenomena, *Barcelona* 202
Picasso Museum, *Málaga* 208
Picona (La) 121
Picos de Europa, *Asturias* 160
Pimpi (El), *Málaga* 50, 208
Pinhan, *Barcelona* 201
Plácido y Grata, *Seville* 32, 207
Platja De La Patacona, *Valencia* 164
Platja De Ses Illetes, *Formentera* 164
Playa De Moda, *Valencia* 46, 204
Playa El Bollullo, *Tenerife* 166
Playa La Caleta, *Cádiz* 162
Playa La Concha, *San Sebastián* 165
Playa De Los Lances, *Tarifa* 167
Plaza 18, *Vejer de la Frontera* 26, 207
Poppyns, *Valencia* 205
Populart, *Seville* 118, 208
Portlligat 123, 203
Principal (La), *Mallorca* 214
Puestu (El), *Barcelona* 201
Purísima (La) 116

Q

Quimbaya, *Madrid* 196

R

Rafael Andreu 116
Rastro (El), *Madrid* 197
Real Fábrica de Cristales de la Granja, *Real Sitio de San Ildefonso* 199
Real Sitio de San Ildefonso 199
Recinte Modernista de Sant Pau, *Barcelona* 202
Rekondo, *San Sebastián* 54, 211
Restaurante Dunas de Famara, *Lanzarote* 215
Restaurante el Bodegón, *San Vicente de la Barquera* 210
Restaurante Miramar, *Menorca* 214
Restaurante Pasapán, *Segovia* 199
Rianxo 105, 214
Rinconcillo (El), *Seville* 72, 207
Río Oja, *Bilbao* 210
Rosa Cadaqués, *Cadaqués* 203
Rosa del Mar Restaurante, *Mallorca* 214
Rosewood Villa Magna, *Madrid* 28, 196

S

Sala Equis, *Madrid* 198
Salamanca 209
Salzillo, *Murcia* 47, 206
San Sebastián 20, 34, 54, 55, 62, 69, 99, 104, 124, 141, 165, 209–212
San Vicente de la Barquera 210
Santa & Cole, *Barcelona* 17, 31, 90–91, 117, 202
Santa Eulalia, *Barcelona* 201
Santander 58, 82, 135, 209–212
Santiago de Compostela 67, 153, 172, 181, 210
Santo Mauro, *Madrid* 196
Santuario de Arántzazu, *Oñati* 155
Sargadelos, *Cervo* 67, 93, 115, 172, 211
Sastrería (La), *Valencia* 204
Savas, *Madrid* 74, 197
Sebastian Melmoth, *Valencia* 205
Secret du Marais (Le), *Madrid* 198

Segovia 24, 89, 199
Serawa Hotels 39, 206
Ses Escoles, *Ibiza* 213
Seville 32, 33, 48, 72, 95, 132—133, 136, 207—208
Shon Mott, *Barcelona* 201
Sidonia 119
Six Senses Ibiza, *Ibiza* 16, 213
Sociedade Xeral de Autores e Editores HQ, *Santiago de Compostela* 153
Somodó, *Barcelona* 201
Sorzano 27, 209
Sportivo, *Madrid* 103, 198
Studio Jaia, *Mallorca* 192
Suárez Muiños, *Élida* 39
Súper de los Pastores 120

T

Tabacalera Promoción del Arte, *Madrid* 198
Tabanco el Pasaje, *Jerez de la Frontera* 138, 208
Taberna Casa Manteca, *Cádiz* 207
Taberna del Gourmet, *Alicante* 206
Tado, *Madrid* 197
Tarifa 167, 174—175
Tasca 61, *Tenerife* 215
Tenderete Sevilla, *Seville* 118, 208
Tenerife 21, 71, 139, 158—159, 166, 215
Tenerife Espacio de las Artes, *Tenerife* 215
Teresas (Las), *Seville* 48, 208
Three Marks Coffee, *Barcelona* 201
Timanfaya, *Lanzarote* 157
Toma Café, *Madrid* 68, 196
Toni2, *Madrid* 196
Torralbenc, *Menorca* 213
Torres Blancas, *Madrid* 149
Treku, *Zarautz* 188, 211

U

Ulisses, *Menorca* 61, 214
Última Parada, *Corçà* 203
Universidad Laboral de Gijón, *Gijón* 135, 212
Urso Hotel & Spa, *Madrid* 196

V

Vachata, *Valencia* 64, 205
Valencia
   STAY 32, 204
   EAT & DRINK 45, 46, 64, 77, 81, 85, 193, 204—205,
   SHOP 92, 99, 205
   DO 147, 164, 170—171, 205
Valladolid 25, 199
Vejer de la Frontera 26, 130, 207
Víctor Montes, *Bilbao* 210
Vigo 163, 172—173, 191, 211, 212
Villa Magdalena, *San Sebastián* 212
Villa Riu Blanc, *Jávea* 25, 206
Villademoros 209
Vinostrum, *Valencia* 204
Viu Empordà, *Costa Brava* 203

W

Working in the Redwoods, *Barcelona* 201

X

Xemei, *Barcelona* 201
Xiringuito Postiguet, *Alicante* 206
Xocolata Jolonch 118
Xoriguer Mahon Gin 120

Y

Yours Boutique Hotel, *Valencia* 32, 204
Yurbban Trafalgar, 200

Z

Zarautz 188, 211
Zero Gravity, *Tarifa* 175

ACKNOWLEDGEMENTS

MONOCLE

Editorial Director & Chairman
Tyler Brûlé

Editor in Chief
Andrew Tuck

Head of Book Publishing
Joe Pickard

Deputy Editor
Molly Price

Assistant Editor
Amy van den Berg

Creative Director
Richard Spencer Powell

Art Director
Sam Brogan

Junior Designer
Oli Kellar

Photography Director
Matthew Beaman

Assistant Photography Editor
Amara Eno

Junior Photography Editor
Kamila Lozinska

Production Director
Jacqueline Deacon

Production Manager
Sarah Kramer

SPECIAL THANKS

César Fernández Tejero
Enrique Jerez
María Jose Alasa
Sagra Maceira de Rosen
Xabier de la Maza
Juan Muñoz
Jayne Nelson
Enric Pastor
Amy Richardson
Nicolas Yllera
Carlos Zamora

WRITERS

Liam Aldous
Ivan Carvalho
Claudia Jacob
Francheska Melendez
Polina Morova
Joe Pickard
Molly Price
Saul Taylor
Andrew Tuck
Hester Underhill
Amy van den Berg
Julia Webster Ayuso

RESEARCHERS

Alexandra Aldea
Mashal Butt
Leila El Shennawy
Conor McCann

PRINCIPAL PHOTOGRAPHERS

Luís Diaz Diaz
Víctor Garrido
Anna Huix
Anthony Perez
Markel Redondo
Ben Roberts
Bacon Studio

PHOTOGRAPHERS

Mark Arrigo
Gregori Civera
Silvia Conde
Pelle Crepin
Ana Cuba
David Fernandez
José Hevia
Nikolas Koenig
Salva Lopez
Benjamin McMahon
Nathalie Mohadjer
Miren Pastor
Laura Tomás
Mathilde Viegas
Philip Vile

IMAGE LIBRARIES

View Pictures
Getty Images
Alamy

ILLUSTRATORS

Owen Gatley
Matteo Riva

ABOUT MONOCLE

Join our club

In 2007, MONOCLE was launched as a monthly magazine briefing on global affairs, business, design and more. Today we have a thriving print business, a radio station, shops, cafés, books, films and events. At our core is the simple belief that there will always be a place for a brand that is committed to telling fresh stories, delivering good journalism and being on the ground around the world. We're Zürich and London-based and have bureaux in Hong Kong, Tokyo, Toronto and Los Angeles.
Subscribe at *monocle.com*

Monocle magazine

MONOCLE magazine is published 10 times a year, including two double issues (July/August and December/January). We also have annual specials: THE FORECAST and two editions of THE ENTREPRENEURS. Look out for our seasonal weekly newspapers too.

Monocle 24 radio

Our round-the-clock online radio station delivers global news and shows covering foreign affairs, urbanism, business, culture, food and drink, design and print media. You can listen live or download shows from monocle.com/radio – or wherever you get your podcasts.

Books

Since 2013, MONOCLE has been publishing books such as this one, covering a range of topics from home design to how to live a gentler life. All our books are available on our website, through our distributor Thames & Hudson or at all good bookshops.

Monocle Minute

MONOCLE's smartly appointed family of newsletters comes from our team of editors and bureaux chiefs around the world. From the daily *Monocle Minute* to the *Monocle Weekend Editions* and our weekly *On Design* special, sign up to get the latest in lifestyle, affairs and design, straight to your inbox every day.

MONOCLE